BREAK FREE FROM RELATIONSHIP ANXIETY & OVERTHINKING

BREAK FREE FROM RELATIONSHIP ANXIETY & OVERTHINKING

Silence Your Inner Critic and
Transform Anxious Thoughts into
Self-Compassion and Confidence with
These Tools for Emotional Growth

Cynthia Shepherd

McLonergan Publishing

ISBN 979-8-9916684-0-8
ISBN 979-8-9916684-1-5 (pbk)
ISBN 979-8-9916684-2-2 (ebook)
Printed in The United States of America

This publication is designed to provide accurate and authoritative information in regards to the subject matter covered. It is sold with the understanding that neither the author nor the publisher is engaged in rendering medical, psycological, legal, investment, accounting, or other professional services. While the author has used their best efforts in preparing this book, they make no representations or warranties with respect to the accuracy or completeness of the contents of this book and specifically disclaim any implied warranties of merchantability or fitness for a particular purpose. No warranty may be created or extended by sales representatives or written sales materials. The advice and strategies contained herein may not be suitable for your situation. You should consult with a professional when appropriate. The author shall not be liable for any loss of profit or any other commercial damages, including but not limited to special, incidental, consequential, personal, or other damages.

Please consult a licensed professional before attempting any techniques outlined in this book. The names of case study subjects featured in this book have been changed to protect privacy.

CONTENTS

INTRODUCTION

The first time relationship anxiety took hold of me I found myself spiraling into thoughts of inadequacy and fear. My partner had been distant for a few days, and my mind raced with worst-case scenarios. I questioned my worth, replayed every conversation, and dissected every interaction for signs of impending doom. The anxiety was paralyzing, and I felt utterly alone in my struggle.

This book is born out of those nights and many others like them. Its purpose is to offer a compassionate guide for those grappling with relationship anxiety and overthinking. It empowers you to reclaim your emotional well-being and build healthier, more fulfilling relationships.

My vision for this book is simple yet profound: to transform your anxious thoughts into self-compassion and confidence. We will explore the root causes of relationship anxiety, provide practical tools to quiet your inner critic, and offer strategies to build a foundation of self-love and resilience.

You might be wondering if this book is for you. If you struggle with low self-esteem, identify as a highly sensitive person (HSP), or are navigating the complexities of early romantic relationships, this book is for you. If you have a history of difficult or traumatic relationships, experience general anxiety, or are recovering from a recent breakup or divorce, this book will offer you solace and guidance. Whether you have attachment issues stemming from childhood or social anxiety affecting your romantic life, you'll find the tools and insights you need here.

This book includes several key features designed to support your journey. You will find clear explanations of relationship anxiety's root causes, practical tools to silence your inner critic and strategies for self-compassion and confidence. We'll delve into methods for managing emotional overwhelm and offer trauma-informed approaches for healing past wounds. You'll also find guidance on building healthy relationship foundations and interactive exercises to engage deeply with the material and create lasting change.

My connection to this topic runs deep. Over three decades ago, I struggled with the effects of personality disorders within my family, leading to severe anxiety in my relationships. Determined to overcome these challenges, I sought the help of psychologists and therapists and immersed myself in studying psychology, neuroscience, and relationship dynamics. Through years of research and personal experience, I developed a unique approach to managing relationship anxiety that blends scientific insights with practical strategies.

What sets this book apart is its holistic approach. We will address your mental, emotional, and physical well-being. The content is diverse and inclusive, offering strategies to overcome common roadblocks and advice on when to seek professional help. You'll also find tools for maintaining your progress long after reading.

Working through this book, you'll learn to quiet your inner critic and approach relationships more confidently. You'll navigate challenges with resilience and cultivate self-love and emotional freedom. The ultimate goal is to transform your relationships with yourself and others, opening new possibilities for love, connection, and personal fulfillment.

In the following pages, you'll find a compassionate companion guiding you through the complexities of relationship anxiety and overthinking. Remember, you are not alone in this journey. Together, we will explore, learn, and grow, creating a life filled with healthier relationships and a stronger sense of self.

Here's to your journey of transformation and emotional growth.

CHAPTER ONE

Understanding Relationship Anxiety and Overthinking

In the stillness of night, have you ever found yourself wide awake, your mind replaying a conversation with your partner on an endless loop? Every word, every pause, every subtle expression becomes a subject of intense scrutiny. I've been there, countless times, analyzing each interaction to the point of exhaustion, convinced that one misstep could unravel the entire relationship. This constant state of hypervigilance and overthinking isn't just tiring—it's a hallmark of relationship anxiety that can erode your peace and connection over time. It wasn't until I began to understand the nature of these thought patterns that I started to find some respite. In this chapter, we'll explore the roots of relationship anxiety and overthinking, shining a light on these often misunderstood issues. By recognizing these patterns in your own life and understanding their origins, you'll be taking the first crucial steps towards breaking free from their grip and fostering healthier, more secure relationships.

The Anatomy of Relationship Anxiety

Relationship anxiety can feel like a constant storm brewing inside you. It's that nagging worry that something will go wrong, even when everything seems fine. This type of anxiety manifests in various ways. Physically, you might experience an increased heart rate, sweating, or even stomachaches. These symptoms can make you feel on edge and unable to relax, especially in situations involving your partner. Emotionally, you might find yourself in constant worry, continually fearing abandonment or rejection. This fear can be overwhelming, making it difficult to enjoy the present moment or feel secure in your relationship. Behaviorally, relationship anxiety often leads to seeking constant reassurance from your partner or avoiding certain situations altogether because they trigger your anxiety. You might find yourself compulsively checking your phone for messages or overanalyzing every interaction, looking for signs of something wrong.

Several common triggers can lead to relationship anxiety. One significant trigger is insecure attachment styles, which often develop in childhood. If you grew up in an environment where your emotional needs weren't consistently met, you might have learned to doubt your self-worth and fear abandonment. Past relationship traumas can also contribute to relationship anxiety. If you have been hurt or betrayed before, it's natural to fear that it will happen again. This fear can make you hyper-vigilant, always looking for signs of trouble. The fear of vulnerability and intimacy is another common trigger. Opening up to someone and allowing yourself to be vulnerable can be terrifying, especially if you fear getting hurt. Lastly, low self-esteem and self-worth issues can fuel relationship anxiety. When you don't believe you are worthy of love and respect, doubting your partner's feelings and intentions is easy.

Understanding the psychological mechanisms behind relationship anxiety can help you manage it more effectively. One key mechanism is the fight-or-flight response, which is your body's natural reaction to perceived threats. In the context of relationships, this response can be triggered by fears of rejection or abandonment, leading to anxiety and defensive behaviors. Cognitive distortions, such as catastrophizing and overgeneralization, also play a role. Catastrophizing involves imagining the worst-case scenario, while overgeneralization means applying one negative experience to all future situations. These distortions can make minor issues feel like significant threats. Childhood experiences and attachment styles also have a profound impact on relationship anxiety. If you grew up in an unstable or emotionally neglectful environment, you might have developed an anxious attachment style, which makes you more prone to relationship anxiety.

Self-awareness is a powerful tool for managing relation-ship anxiety. By becoming more aware of your behaviors, thoughts, and feelings, you can start to identify patterns and triggers. Practicing mindfulness can help you stay present and observe your thoughts without judgment, giving you space to respond rather than react. Journaling prompts for self-reflection can also be beneficial. Writing down your thoughts and feelings can help you gather clarity and insight into your anxiety. Identify personal triggers and patterns by reflecting on past experiences and current behaviors. This awareness can empower you to make conscious changes and take proactive steps toward managing your relationship anxiety.

How Overthinking Sabotages Your Relationships

Overthinking is like a relentless loop that can feel impossible to break. It begins innocuously enough—a text that takes too long to receive a response, a comment that seems slightly off. Before you know it, you analyze every word and action of your partner. You start imagining worst-case scenarios, convinced that something is wrong. This thinking can create a negative feedback loop, reinforcing your fears and anxieties. Seeking constant reassurance becomes a way to cope, but it often backfires. Your partner might feel overwhelmed by your need for validation, leading to tension and misunderstandings. This cycle can quickly become exhausting for both parties, eroding the foundation of trust and security in the relationship.

The impact of overthinking on communication is profound. When you find yourself trapped in a cycle of overthinking, it becomes difficult to express your true feelings openly. You might hesitate, fearing that your words will be misinterpreted or that you will appear needy or insecure. Misinterpreting your partner's actions and words is another common consequence. You might read too much into a simple comment or gesture, assuming it has a deeper, more negative meaning. Misunderstanding can create unnecessary conflicts;

your partner might feel accused or misunderstood. Lack of clear communication can cause frustration, making resolving issues and building a solid connection more difficult.

Overthinking takes a significant emotional toll on a relationship. The constant worry and stress can lead to emotional burnout, where you feel drained and unable to enjoy the relationship. This burnout affects both individuals, as your partner might also feel the strain of your anxiety and need for reassurance. The increased anxiety and stress can make it difficult to relax and enjoy each other's company, leading to a reduced sense of emotional intimacy. You might find it hard to feel close and connected when your mind always races with anxious thoughts. The emotional exhaustion can make it challenging to invest in the relationship, as you might feel too overwhelmed to address issues or nurture your bond.

Breaking the overthinking cycle requires practical strategies to help you manage your thoughts and emotions. Mindfulness meditation techniques can be incredibly effective in calming your mind and bringing you back to the present moment. Simple practices like focused breathing or body scanning can help you become more aware of your thoughts without getting caught up in them. Cognitive-behavioral strategies can also be helpful. Noticing negative thoughts and replacing them with more balanced, realistic ones can reduce the power of overthinking. Setting specific times for worry can be another useful approach. Instead of allowing anxious thoughts to dominate your entire day, designate a particular time to address your worries. This practice can help you contain your anxiety and prevent it from spilling into every aspect of your life.

Incorporating these strategies into your daily routine can make a remarkable difference. For example, if you find yourself spiraling into anxious thoughts after a conversation with your partner, take a moment to practice mindfulness. Focus on your breath, and try to observe your thoughts without judgment. Remind yourself that not every thought is a fact, and challenge any negative assumptions you might make. Keep a journal where you can write and analyze your worries later. This practice can give you a clearer outlook and be helpful in pattern recognition. These actions can gradually reduce the hold that overthinking has on your life and relationships, paving the way for a more balanced and fulfilling connection with your partner.

Identifying Your Inner Critic

The inner critic is that relentless voice in your head that never seems to miss an opportunity to point out your flaws and shortcomings. It sometimes whispers that you aren't good enough, your partner will leave, or you don't deserve love. This voice contributes significantly to relationship anxiety by fueling negative self-talk, self-doubt, and insecurity. When your inner critic is in control, it's easy to spiral into a cycle of fear and doubt, questioning every action and word. This relentless negativity can make it challenging to feel confident and secure in your relationship as you constantly battle these undermining thoughts.

The origins of the inner critic are often rooted in childhood experiences and parental criticism. If you grew up in an environment where love and approval were conditional, you might have internalized these critical voices. Society also plays a role, with its unrealistic expectations and pressures to conform to specific standards. Media portrayals of perfect relationships and unattainable beauty can make you feel inadequate, feeding the inner critic. Past relationship experiences, especially those involving betrayal or rejection, can further bolster this negative voice. These experiences create a mental script that repeats itself, making it hard to trust and feel secure in new relationships.

Recognizing the inner critic is the first step in quieting it. Start by tracking your negative thoughts through journaling. Whenever you catch yourself thinking critically, write it down. This practice helps you become more aware of the patterns and triggers of your inner critic. Mindfulness practices can also be beneficial. Spend a few minutes each day observing your thoughts without judgment. Notice when the inner critic speaks up and try to understand its source. Self-reflection questions, such as "What is my inner critic saying?" or "Where did this thought come from?" can provide deeper insights into your inner dialogue.

Once you've identified your inner critic, you can silence it using several techniques. Positive affirmations are a powerful tool. Create a list of affirmations that counter your inner critic's negative messages. For example, if your inner critic says, "You're not good enough," an affirmation might be, "I am worthy of love and respect." Repeat these affirmations daily, especially when you notice your inner critic becoming loud. Cognitive restructuring is another effective strategy. This involves challenging and reframing negative thoughts. Ask yourself if there is evidence to support your inner critic's claims. Often, you'll find that these thoughts are based on irrational fears rather than facts.

Developing self-compassion is crucial in managing the inner critic. Treat yourself with the same understanding and compassion you would offer a friend. When you catch yourself being self-critical, pause and consider how you would respond if a friend shared the same concern. Practice self-compassionate journaling by writing supportive and encouraging letters to yourself. Recognize that making mistakes and experiencing setbacks are part of being human. Embrace your imperfections and appreciate your efforts, even when things don't go as planned.

Incorporating these strategies into your daily routine can gradually diminish the power of your inner critic. For instance, if you find yourself doubting your worth after a disagreement with your partner, take a moment to practice mindfulness. Observe your thoughts and remind yourself that it's okay to feel upset. Challenge any irrational thoughts and replace them with positive affirmations. Reflect on the situation with self-compassion, acknowledging your feelings, and reminding yourself that it's normal to have conflicts in relationships. These techniques, if applied consistently, can create a more supportive and loving inner dialogue, reducing anxiety and building a stronger sense of self-worth.

The Impact of Past Traumas on Current Relationships

Past relationship traumas can cast long shadows over current relationships, often influencing behaviors and emotions in ways that are hard to pinpoint. Trust issues are among the most common manifestations of past trauma. Carrying that pain into new relationships is natural if you've been betrayed or hurt. You might doubt your partner's intentions, even when no evidence supports your fears. This mistrust can create a barrier, preventing you from fully opening up and allowing intimacy to flourish. Fear of vulnerability is another significant way past traumas make their presence felt. When you've been hurt deeply, exposing your true self to someone else can be terrifying. You might put up emotional walls, keeping your partner at arm's length to protect yourself from potential pain. Emotional triggers are also prevalent, where seemingly minor events provoke intense emotional reactions. For instance, a phrase or action from your partner might remind you of a past hurt, leading to an overreaction that puzzles you and your partner.

Recognizing the signs that past trauma is affecting your current relationships is crucial for healing. One of the most apparent indicators is the repetition of negative patterns. You might be in a cycle of choosing similar partners or recreating the same conflicts, even though the circumstances differ. This pattern often stems from unresolved issues and unhealed wounds. Overreacting to minor issues is another red flag. Small disagreements or misunderstandings can escalate quickly, fueled by unresolved emotions from past traumas. This overreaction can strain the relationship, creating a volatile environment where minor issues become major conflicts. Difficulty establishing trust and intimacy is another sign that past trauma is at play. You might struggle to let your guard down, fearing that your partner will hurt you just as others have. This difficulty can prevent the relationship from deepening, leaving both partners feeling disconnected and unfulfilled.

Acknowledging and validating past traumas is a vital step toward healing. It's essential to recognize that your feelings and experiences are valid, even if they are painful. Emotional validation involves accepting your emotions without judgment and understanding that feeling hurt, angry, or scared is okay. Seeking support from loved ones can also be beneficial. Sharing your experiences with trusted friends or family can provide comfort and perspective. They can offer empathy and support, helping you feel less isolated in your pain. Professional therapy and counseling can be invaluable resources. A therapist can provide a safe space to explore traumas and offer tools and techniques to manage their impact on your current relationships.

Healing from past relational traumas requires proactive steps and a commitment to self-care. Trauma-informed therapy approaches, such as EMDR (Eye Movement Desensitization and Reprocessing) or Somatic Experiencing, can help process and release the emotional pain stored in your body. These therapies focus on healing the trauma at its root rather than just addressing the symptoms. Journaling and self-reflection exercises can also be powerful tools for healing. Writing about your experiences and emotions can reveal triggers and patterns, providing you clarity and insight. It allows you to process your feelings in a structured way, making them more manageable. Mindfulness and grounding techniques can help you stay present and calm, reducing the intensity of emotional triggers. Deep breathing, body scanning, and mindfulness meditation can help you stay connected to the present moment, preventing you from getting lost in past pain or future anxieties.

Incorporating these healing techniques into your daily routine can create a foundation for lasting change. For example, if you find yourself triggered by a specific situation, take a moment to practice a grounding technique. Focus on your breath, feel your feet on the ground, and remind yourself that you are safe in the present moment. Journaling can become a nightly ritual, allowing you to reflect on your day and process emotions. Seeking therapy can provide ongoing support and guidance, helping you navigate the complexities of healing from trauma. By taking these steps, you can begin to heal from past wounds, creating space for healthier, more fulfilling relationships in the present.

Unpacking Attachment Styles and Their Effects

Attachment styles are the emotional bonds we form with others, rooted in our earliest interactions with caregivers. These bonds shape how we relate to others throughout our lives. There are four primary attachment styles: secure, anxious, avoidant, and disorganized.

A secure attachment style develops when caregivers consistently respond to a child's needs. This child grows up feeling safe and valued, leading to healthy communication and trust in relationships. They can express their needs and emotions openly and trust their partner to do the same. This balanced dynamic fosters a strong foundation for lasting, fulfilling relationships.

An anxious attachment style forms when caregivers are inconsistently responsive. This inconsistency creates a sense of uncertainty and instability for the child, leading to a fear of abandonment and a constant need for reassurance. As adults, individuals with an anxious attachment style often feel clingy and insecure in their relationships. They may worry excessively about their partner's feelings and question their worth, leading to behaviors that can strain the relationship. This constant need for validation can make maintaining a balanced and healthy connection with their partner difficult.

Avoidant attachment arises when caregivers are emotionally unavailable or dismissive. These children learn to rely on themselves and suppress their emotional needs to avoid disappointment. As adults, they tend to maintain emotional distance and find it challenging to commit to relationships. They might appear aloof or detached, prioritizing independence over intimacy. This emotional distance can create a barrier to deep connections, leaving both partners feeling unfulfilled and disconnected. Avoidant individuals often struggle to express their emotions and may avoid situations that require vulnerability.

Disorganized attachment is a result of caregivers who are both a source of comfort and fear, often due to abusive or neglectful behavior. Disorganized attachment creates a confusing and chaotic emotional experience for the child. As adults, individuals with a disorganized attachment style exhibit erratic and unpredictable relationship behaviors. They may oscillate between seeking closeness and pushing their partner away, leading to confusion and instability. This inconsistency can be challenging for both partners, creating a volatile and unpredictable relationship dynamic. Trust and emotional safety are hard to establish in such relationships.

Self-assessment tools can be incredibly useful in identifying your attachment style. An attachment-style quiz can provide valuable insights into your relationship patterns and behaviors. These quizzes often contain questions about your feelings and reactions in different relational scenarios. Journaling prompts for self-reflection can also help you explore your attachment style. Consider questions like, "How do I typically react when my partner is distant?" or "What do I feel when I'm emotionally close to someone?" Reflecting on your responses can reveal underlying patterns and better help you understand your attachment style.

Moving towards a secure attachment style involves several strategies. Building trust and emotional intimacy is crucial. Secure attachment means being open and honest with your partner about your feelings and needs and trusting them to reciprocate. Effective communication is another critical component. Practice active listening, express your needs clearly, and respond to your partner with empathy and understanding. Seeking therapy for deeper issues can also be immensely beneficial. A therapist can help you work through past traumas and attachment-related challenges, providing tools and techniques to develop healthier relational patterns.

Consider incorporating these strategies into your daily interactions. For example, if you feel anxious about your partner's delayed response, take a moment to practice deep breathing and remind yourself of your partner's consistent behavior. Communicate your feelings calmly, expressing your needs without demanding reassurance. If you're avoidant, open up about your day and share more personal thoughts, even if it feels uncomfortable. This gradual openness can help build intimacy and trust. Working through these strategies consistently can help you develop a more secure attachment style, fostering healthier and more fulfilling relationships.

Recognizing the Signs of Unhealthy Relationship Dynamics

Unhealthy relationship dynamics can be insidious, often creeping in slowly until they become the norm. The characteristics of such relationships are varied but can be broadly categorized. A lack of communication is a significant red flag. When partners fail to openly share their thoughts, feelings, and concerns, misunderstandings fester, and emotional distance grows. It's about talking and engaging in meaningful dialogue where both parties feel heard and understood. Emotional manipulation is another hallmark of unhealthy relationships. Emotional manipulation can take many forms, such as guilt-tripping, gaslighting, or using affection as a bargaining chip. Manipulative behaviors create an imbalance of power, making one partner feel controlled or coerced. Codependency, where one partner relies excessively on the other for emotional support and validation, can also be detrimental. This dynamic stifles individual growth and fosters an unhealthy level of dependency.

Common signs indicating that a relationship might be unhealthy include constant arguments and conflicts. Disagreements are a normal part of any relationship, but they suggest deeper issues when they occur daily. Frequent conflicts can leave both partners feeling drained and emotionally battered. Feeling consistently anxious or on edge around your partner is another warning sign. Relationships should be a source of comfort and security, not stress and fear. If you find yourself walking on eggshells, it's a signal that something is amiss. A loss of individual identity is also telling. Both partners maintain their sense of self and personal interests in a healthy relationship. It may be due to an unhealthy dynamic if you've lost yourself or cannot pursue your passions.

The impact of unhealthy relationships on mental health is profound. Increased anxiety and depression are common, as the constant stress and emotional turmoil take their toll. The erosion of self-esteem is another consequence. Your partner consistently belittling you or ignoring your needs can make you question your worth. Emotional exhaustion is a frequent outcome. Constantly dealing with conflict, manipulation, or emotional neglect can leave you feeling depleted and unable to cope with other aspects of life. This exhaustion can affect your work, social life, and overall well-being, creating a vicious cycle of stress and despair.

Addressing and improving unhealthy relationship dynamics requires both awareness and action. Setting boundaries is crucial. Clear, firm boundaries help protect your emotional well-being and establish acceptable behaviors. Communicating these boundaries to your partner and consistently enforcing them is essential. Seeking couples therapy can also be beneficial. A trained therapist can provide a neutral space to explore issues and facilitate healthier communication patterns. Therapy can help both partners understand their roles in the dynamic and work towards a more balanced relationship. Practicing self-care and self-compassion is equally essential. Engaging in enjoyable and relaxing activities can help replenish your emotional reserves. Self-compassion involves treating yourself with kindness and understanding, especially when dealing with relationship challenges.

For example, imagine a couple where one partner constantly belittles the other, leading to frequent arguments and emotional distress. The belittled partner may feel anxious and lose their sense of self-worth. Recognizing this dynamic is the first step. Setting boundaries, such as stating that belittling comments are unacceptable, can help. Seeking couples therapy can provide a space to address the underlying issues and improve communication. Engaging in self-care activities, like spending time with supportive friends or pursuing a hobby, can help rebuild self-esteem and reduce emotional exhaustion.

Recognizing these signs and taking proactive steps can shift the dynamic towards a healthier, more balanced relationship. It's about creating an environment where both partners feel valued, respected, and supported. This journey requires commitment and effort, but the rewards of a healthy, fulfilling relationship are well worth it. Remember, you deserve to feel safe and cherished in your relationships.

CHAPTER TWO

Building Self-Awareness and Self-Compassion

Understanding yourself is the cornerstone of personal growth. Self-reflection is turning your attention inward to examine your thoughts, feelings, and behaviors. This process allows you to gain deeper insights into who you are and why you act the way you do. Reflecting on past relationship patterns is particularly important. By examining your past relationships, you can identify recurring behaviors and emotional triggers that may affect your current relationship. For example, you might notice a pattern of avoiding conflict, which could stem from a fear of rejection. Understanding these patterns enables you to make conscious changes and break free from unhealthy cycles.

Identifying recurring emotional triggers is another crucial aspect of self-reflection. Emotional triggers are specific events or situations that provoke intense emotional reactions. By recognizing these triggers, you can better understand the underlying issues that cause them. For instance, if you find yourself feeling anxious whenever your partner is late, it might be linked to past experiences of being let down or abandoned. Understanding personal values and beliefs is also essential. Your values and beliefs shape your actions and decisions. Reflecting on what truly matters to you can help you align your behavior with your core values, leading to more authentic and fulfilling relationships.

There are various methods of self-reflection that you can incorporate into your daily life. Meditation is a powerful way to turn inward and observe your thoughts without judgment. Even just a few minutes of meditation daily can help you become more aware of your inner landscape. Journaling prompts are another effective tool. Writing down your thoughts and feelings allows you to externalize them, making them easier to analyze. Some prompts you might consider include, "What did I learn about myself today?" or "How did I handle my emotions in a challenging situation?" Guided self-reflection exercises, such as those led by a therapist or through self-help books, can also provide structure and support as you explore your inner world.

Incorporating self-reflection into your daily routine doesn't have to be time-consuming. Setting aside a specific time each day for reflection can make it a regular habit. This could be first thing in the morning as you lay in bed or at the end of the day as you turn in for the night. Creating a conducive environment for introspection is also essential. Find a quiet, comfortable space where you can reflect without distractions. This could be a cozy corner in your home, a peaceful park, or a quiet room in your office. Reflection tools like journals or apps can help you stay organized and consistent. Some apps offer guided reflection exercises and prompts, making starting easier.

To guide your self-reflection process, consider asking yourself specific questions and diving deeper into your thoughts and feelings. For example, "What did I learn about myself today?" encourages you to reflect on your daily experiences and draw insights from them. "How did I handle my emotions in a challenging situation?" helps you assess your emotional responses and identify areas for improvement. "What are my strengths, and how can I use them more effectively?" prompts you to recognize your unique qualities and consider leveraging them in your relationships and daily life.

Reflecting on your thoughts, feelings, and behaviors can help you gain insights into yourself and your relationships. This self-awareness is the first step toward building self-compassion and making positive changes in your life. The transformative power of self-reflection can bring hope for a brighter, more fulfilling future.

Daily Mindfulness Practices for Emotional Regulation

Mindfulness is a powerful tool that can help you stay grounded and present, especially when anxiety and overthinking take over. At its core, mindfulness is about staying present in the moment and observing your thoughts and feelings without judgment. This practice can create a space between you and your reactions, allowing you to respond more thoughtfully rather than impulsively. It's about becoming aware of your internal landscape and learning to navigate it calmly and clearly.

One of the simplest yet most effective mindfulness practices is deep breathing. This exercise involves taking slow, deliberate breaths, which can reduce anxiety and help calm your nervous system. The simplicity of this practice makes it accessible to everyone, regardless of their daily schedule or location. Start by finding a quiet place to sit comfortably. Close your eyes and take a deep breath through your nose, allowing your abdomen to expand. Hold your breath briefly, then slowly exhale through your mouth. Repeat this process several times, focusing solely on your breath coming in and out of your body. You can practice this anywhere, whether at home, work, or even in a stressful situation.

Another mindfulness technique is body scanning, which involves paying attention to different parts of your body, one at a time. Begin by lying down or sitting comfortably. Close your eyes and take a few deep breaths to center yourself. Start at the top of your head and slowly work your way down to your toes, focusing on each body part and noticing any sensations you might feel. If you encounter areas of tension or discomfort, breathe into them and try to release the tension with each exhale. This practice helps you become more attuned to your physical state and can be particularly useful for releasing built-up stress.

Walking is another effective way to practice mindfulness. This exercise involves paying close attention to your steps, focusing on each foot landing on the ground. Find a quiet place without distractions where you can walk. As you walk, pay attention to the feeling and movement of your legs and the rhythm of your breath. If you find your mind wandering, gently focus back on the act of walking. This practice can be refreshing, clearing your mind and connecting with the present moment

The benefits of mindfulness for managing anxiety and stress are well-documented. Regular mindfulness practice can help reduce anxiety and stress by calming the mind and body. It improves emotional resilience, allowing you to handle life's challenges easily. Mindfulness also enhances self-awareness, helping you understand your thoughts and emotions better, which can lead to more thoughtful responses and healthier relationship.

Incorporating mindfulness into your daily routine doesn't have to be complicated. You can practice mindfulness during meals by paying attention to your food's taste, texture, and smell. This not only enhances your eating experience but also helps you stay present. Using mindfulness breaks during work or study can also be beneficial. Take a few minutes to step away from your tasks, close your eyes, and focus on your breath. This can help reset your mind and improve concentration. Mindful listening in conversations is another way to incorporate mindfulness. When talking to someone, give them your full attention, listen without interrupting, and notice their words and body language.

Integrating these mindfulness practices into your daily life can create a more balanced and peaceful mind. Whether dealing with the stress of a busy day, navigating complex emotions, or simply seeking a moment of calm, mindfulness can provide the tools to stay grounded and present.

Challenging Negative Self-Talk

Negative self-talk can be like a dark cloud hanging over your head, casting shadows on your confidence and self-worth. Constantly telling yourself you aren't good enough creates deep self-doubt. This doubt seeps into every aspect of your life, making you question your abilities and decisions. In relationships, negative self-talk can fuel anxiety and overthinking, leading you to second-guess your partner's feelings and actions. You might find yourself wondering if they genuinely care about you or if they are secretly dissatisfied. This constant questioning can strain the relationship, as your need for reassurance might come off as insecurity or mistrust. Over time, negative self-talk erodes your self-worth, making it difficult to believe you deserve love and respect. This cycle can be exhausting, leaving you feeling emotionally drained and disconnected from your partner.

Cognitive restructuring is a powerful technique to challenge and change negative self-talk. The first step is identifying cognitive distortions and irrational patterns reinforcing negative thinking. Common distortions include catastrophizing, where you imagine the worst-case scenario, and overgeneralization, where you apply one negative experience to all future situations. Once you recognize these distortions, you can reframe your negative thoughts. Reframing involves looking at a problem from a different perspective and challenging the validity of your negative beliefs. For example, if you think, "I'm always messing things up," challenge this thought by considering times when you succeeded or handled situations well. Practicing positive affirmations is another effective strategy. Affirmations are positive statements that counteract negative self-talk. By repeating affirmations such as "I am worthy of love" or "I am capable and strong," you can gradually replace negative beliefs with more empowering ones.

To put these strategies into practice, consider starting a thought log. In this log, write down any negative thoughts that come to mind throughout the day. Next to each thought, identify the cognitive distortion and write a positive counter-statement. For instance, if you think, "My partner must be upset with me because they didn't text back immediately," identify the distortion (e.g., mind-reading) and counter it with, "There could be many reasons for the delay, and it doesn't necessarily mean they are upset with me." This routine helps you become more aware of your thought patterns and provides a structured way to challenge them.

You can also incorporate daily affirmations into your morning or evening routine. Spend a few minutes each day repeating affirmations that resonate with you, silently or out loud. Over time, these positive statements can help shift your mindset and build confidence.

Real-life examples powerfully illustrate the transformative effect of challenging negative self-talk. Take Sarah, a 28-year-old nutritionist who had always struggled with feelings of inadequacy in her relationships. Sarah shared that she barely spoke on her third date with Alex, convinced her thoughts weren't worth sharing. She had no confidence that anything she would say would be at all interesting to him.

This pattern continued for weeks. Sarah would spend hours preparing witty anecdotes before their dates, only to clam up in Alex's presence. She'd analyze every interaction afterward, berating herself for perceived missteps, convinced that she was just not interesting enough.

Recognizing her spiraling anxiety, Sarah began cognitive restructuring exercises. She kept a thought log, jotting down her automatic negative thoughts and examining the evidence for and against them. Sarah realized that Alex consistently showed interest in her ideas and experiences, contradicting her belief that she was boring.

She practiced reframing her thoughts: "I may not have traveled the world, but my perspective is unique and valuable." Sarah created daily affirmations, repeating them in the mirror each morning: "I am worthy of love and connection just as I am."

Gradually, Sarah noticed a shift. When Alex asked about her day during a dinner date, she shared a challenging work situation without self-deprecation. She even found herself laughing genuinely at her own joke, and was delighted with Alex's response of laughter and warmth.

As Sarah's confidence grew, so did her ability to connect authentically. She began sharing her passion for local art, even inviting Alex to a gallery opening. To her surprise, he was fascinated by her knowledge and perspective.

Six months later, Sarah relayed the story that Alex said he loved how she had opened up, and her thoughts and ideas were what drew him to her in the first place. Sarah realized how far she'd come from those early days of self-doubt. By challenging her negative self-talk, she had not only transformed her self-perception but also cultivated a deeper, more genuine connection in her relationship.

In another case, John, a 35-year-old software engineer, found himself in a constant state of anxiety about his relationship with Maria. One Friday evening, Maria mentioned she was going out with coworkers. John's mind immediately went into overdrive wondering why she didn't invite him to go with her.

Throughout the night, John checked his phone obsessively, interpreting Maria's lack of messages as confirmation of his fears. By the time she returned home, John was a bundle of nerves, barely able to mask his distress.

Recognizing this pattern, John started employing cognitive behavioral techniques. He began by keeping a thought record. Each time he felt anxious about Maria's actions, he wrote down his automatic thoughts:

"Maria's out late. She must be flirting with someone else." "She hasn't texted in hours. She's probably realizing she doesn't want to be with me."

John then challenged these thoughts with evidence:

"Maria has always been faithful and transparent about her plans." "She mentioned it was a team bonding event, and she's likely engaged in activities."

He practiced reframing his thoughts:

"Maria deserves to have fun with her colleagues. This doesn't threaten our relationship." "Her enjoying time with others doesn't diminish her feelings for me."

John also started mindfulness meditation to help him stay present rather than spiral into worst-case scenarios. When anxious thoughts arose, he acknowledged them without judgment and gently redirected his focus to his breath or a calming visualization.

Over time, John noticed a significant change. When Maria mentioned another work event, instead of panicking, John found himself genuinely interested and asked her questions about it. He was surprised to note a feeling of lightness and calm as he listened to Maria's excitement about the event.

As weeks passed, John found himself worrying less and enjoying their time together more. He was present during conversations, no longer distracted by imagined scenarios. Their relationship deepened, built on a foundation of trust and open communication.

John's experience demonstrates that with consistent effort and the right techniques, it's possible to overcome the trap of overthinking and build a healthier, more secure relationship. By challenging his negative thoughts and fostering open dialogue, John not only eased his own anxiety but also strengthened his bond with Maria.

Understanding Your Emotional Triggers

Emotional triggers are specific events, words, or situations that provoke intense emotional reactions. These reactions often seem disproportionate to the triggering event, catching you off guard and overwhelming you. Understanding your emotional triggers is crucial because they can significantly impact your relationships and overall well-being. By identifying the sources of these intense reactions, patterns in your emotional responses will emerge so you can manage them more constructively. For instance, if you feel inexplicably angry when your partner is late, it might be rooted in past experiences of feeling neglected or abandoned. Recognizing these patterns helps you understand the underlying issues at play.

One practical method to identify your emotional triggers is to keep an emotion diary. In this diary, jot down moments when you experience strong emotional reactions. Note the situation, your feelings, and any thoughts accompanying those feelings. Over time, you'll begin to see patterns emerge, making it easier to pinpoint specific triggers. Reflecting on past emotional reactions is also valuable. Remember when you felt intensely angry, sad, or anxious? What was happening at the time? How did you react? What thoughts were running through your mind? This reflection can provide insights into recurring themes and triggers. Seeking feedback from trusted friends or therapists can offer an outside perspective. Sometimes, those close to you can see patterns that you might miss. Discussing your experiences with someone you trust can help you better understand your emotional triggers.

Unaddressed emotional triggers can wreak havoc on relationships. Miscommunication and misunderstandings are common when emotional triggers are at play. Your partner might not understand why you react strongly to specific situations, leading to confusion and frustration. These misunderstandings can escalate conflicts, making it difficult to resolve issues and creating a cycle of tension and discord. Emotional distancing is another consequence of unrecognized triggers. If you frequently experience intense emotional reactions, you might start to withdraw from your partner to protect yourself from further distress. This distancing can create a barrier to intimacy, leaving both partners feeling disconnected and isolated.

Managing and coping with emotional triggers involves several strategies. Grounding techniques can be particularly effective. When triggered, take a moment to ground yourself in the present. Focus on your senses—what you can see, hear, touch, taste, and smell. This practice can help anchor you and prevent your emotions from spiraling out of control. Cognitive-behavioral strategies are also helpful. Challenge the thoughts that arise when you're triggered. Ask yourself if these thoughts are based on facts or distorted by past experiences. By reframing these thoughts, you can reduce the intensity of your emotional reactions. Mindfulness practices can help you stay present and observe your emotions without judgment. Regularly practicing mindfulness can develop greater emotional resilience and better manage triggers.

For example, imagine you feel a surge of anxiety whenever your partner doesn't immediately respond to your messages. Start by grounding yourself—focus on the texture of an object nearby, or take a few deep breaths. Then, challenge the thought, "They must be upset with me." Consider other possibilities, such as they might be busy or haven't seen the message yet. Lastly, practice mindfulness by observing your anxiety without judgment. Acknowledge it, but don't let it control your actions. Over time, these strategies can help you manage your emotional triggers more effectively, leading to healthier and more balanced relationships.

The Role of Self-Compassion in Healing

Self-compassion is a concept that might seem foreign at first, especially if you are used to being hard on yourself. But it's a powerful tool for emotional healing. At its core, self-compassion involves treating yourself with the kindness and understanding you would offer a friend in distress. When you make a mistake or face a setback, self-compassion encourages you to respond gently rather than berate yourself. This practice is crucial because it creates a safe internal environment where you can acknowledge your vulnerabilities without being overwhelmed. Recognizing shared humanity is also a key component. It is about understanding that everyone makes mistakes and experiences pain, and you are not alone in your struggles. This perspective helps you feel connected to others, reducing feelings of isolation. Finally, practicing mindfulness allows you to observe your thoughts and feelings without judgment, creating space for self-compassion to take root.

The benefits of self-compassion for mental health are profound. One of the most significant advantages is the reduction of self-criticism. When you treat yourself with kindness, you break the cycle of harsh self-judgment that can fuel anxiety and depression. This gentle approach fosters a more positive self-image and enhances emotional resilience, making coping with life's challenges more manageable. Self-compassion also promotes healing and growth by creating an internal atmosphere of acceptance and support. When you are kind to yourself, you are more likely to take constructive steps towards self-improvement rather than being paralyzed by fear of failure. This nurturing environment allows you to learn and grow from your experiences without being weighed down by self-reproach.

To cultivate self-compassion, you can start with simple, actionable exercises. Loving-kindness meditation is a powerful practice that involves sending goodwill and positive intentions to yourself and others. To start, find a quiet place to sit comfortably. Close your eyes and take a few deep breaths. Then, silently repeat phrases like, "Let me find joy, security, wellness, and peace in my life." Gradually extend these wishes to include loved ones, acquaintances, and even people you find challenging. This practice helps foster a sense of compassion and connection. Self-compassionate journaling is another effective exercise. Set aside time each day to write about your experiences, focusing on areas where you can offer yourself kindness and understanding. Reflect on moments of difficulty and how you can respond to yourself with compassion. Practicing self-kindness in daily life is also essential. This can be as simple as taking a break when you feel overwhelmed, speaking to yourself gently, or acknowledging your efforts and achievements.

Real-life examples can illustrate the transformative power of self-compassion. Emily, a 31-year-old elementary school teacher, found herself sitting alone in her apartment on a Friday night, six weeks after her boyfriend of three years, Mark, had ended their relationship. As she scrolled through social media, a photo of Mark at a party with a stunning woman by his side popped up. Emily's chest tightened, and tears welled in her eyes.

Her self-critical thoughts had become Emily's constant companions since the breakup. She replayed every argument, every perceived flaw in herself, convinced that she was solely to blame for the relationship's demise.

One particularly low evening, Emily reached out to her best friend, Sophie, who suggested trying self-compassion exercises. Skeptical but desperate, Emily decided to give it a shot.

She started with a simple self-compassionate journaling exercise. That night, instead of ruminating on her perceived failings, Emily wrote:

"Dear Emily, I know you're hurting right now. It's okay to feel sad and disappointed. Breakups are painful, and your feelings are valid. You did your best in the relationship, and sometimes things don't work out despite our efforts. This doesn't make you a failure. You are worthy of love and happiness, just as you are."

At first, the words felt forced and insincere. But as Emily continued this practice nightly, something began to shift. She started to recognize patterns in her self-talk that were unnecessarily harsh.

One day, while grocery shopping, Emily ran into Mark and his new girlfriend. Her initial reaction was a familiar wave of self-loathing. But then she paused, took a deep breath, and silently told herself, "This is a difficult moment. It's natural to feel hurt and jealous. Be kind to yourself, Emily."

To her surprise, this small act of self-compassion helped her navigate the encounter with more grace than she thought possible. She even managed a genuine smile and brief conversation before excusing herself.

As weeks passed, Emily noticed other changes. When a first date didn't lead to a second, instead of spiraling into self-criticism, she wrote in her journal: "Dating can be disappointing sometimes, but that doesn't reflect on my worth. I'm proud of myself for putting myself out there."

Three months into her self-compassion practice, Emily's friends noticed the change in her, saying she seemed more at peace.

Emily smiled, realizing the truth in her friend's words. She still had moments of sadness about the breakup, but they no longer consumed her. She felt more resilient, more capable of facing her emotions without being overwhelmed by them.

One evening, as Emily wrote her nightly self-compassionate letter, she realized she was writing about her hopes for the future rather than dwelling on past hurts. She felt a warm sense of pride and optimism wash over her. By treating herself with the kindness she'd so readily offer a friend, Emily had not only healed from her breakup but had also cultivated a deeper, more compassionate relationship with herself.

Self-compassion is not just a feel-good concept; it's a practical, assertive approach to emotional healing. You can create an internal environment that supports growth and resilience by treating yourself with kindness, recognizing your shared humanity, and practicing mindfulness. Whether through meditation, journaling, or daily acts of kindness, these practices can help you build a more compassionate relationship with yourself, paving the way for more profound emotional healing and well-being.

Journaling for Self-Discovery

Journaling can be an incredibly powerful tool for self-discovery. It provides a safe space to clarify your thoughts and feelings, helping you understand yourself better. Writing down your thoughts can make abstract feelings more concrete. This clarity can lead to personal growth as you identify patterns and triggers that influence your behavior. For example, you might notice that certain words or actions from your partner trigger feelings of insecurity. By journaling, you can explore these triggers and consider their origins, whether from past relationships or childhood experiences. This self-awareness can guide you in making conscious changes to improve your emotional well-being.

To benefit from journaling, it's important to start with a solid foundation. First, set aside dedicated time for journaling. This could be in the morning to set the tone for your day or in the evening to reflect on your experiences. Consistency is key, so try to journal at the same time each day. Create a safe and comfortable space where you can write without distractions.

This might be a quiet corner of your home or a peaceful spot in a park. Choose a journaling format that suits you. Some people prefer free writing, where they let their thoughts flow without structure. Others might find prompts more helpful, guiding their reflection on specific topics.

Journaling Prompts for Self-Discovery

Prompts can provide direction and depth to your journaling practice. Here are some to consider:

"What are my core values, and how do they influence my actions?" Reflecting on your values can help you understand your motivations and align your actions with what truly matters to you

"What patterns do I notice in my relationships?" Identifying recurring themes in your relationships can reveal underlying issues or strengths.

"How do I typically respond to stress, and what can I learn?" Examining your stress responses can help you develop healthier coping mechanisms.

"What are my strengths, and how can I use them more effectively?" Acknowledging your strengths can boost your confidence and guide you in leveraging them in various aspects of your life.

Overcoming common journaling challenges can make your practice more effective. Writer's block is a frequent obstacle. If you find yourself staring at a blank page, start with a simple prompt or write about your day. The act of writing can help unlock more profound thoughts. Maintaining consistency can also be challenging. To stay on track, set reminders or make journaling a part of your daily routine, like brushing your teeth. It's also important to ensure privacy and security. Use a password-protected digital journal or keep your physical journal in a safe place. Knowing that your thoughts are secure can make it easier to write honestly.

In summary, journaling is a versatile tool that can enhance self-discovery and personal growth. By clarifying your thoughts, identifying patterns and triggers, and facilitating emotional expression, journaling can provide insights that lead to meaningful change. With the right approach and a few practical strategies, you can make journaling a valuable part of your self-care routine. As you continue to explore your inner world, you'll find that this practice helps you understand yourself better and improves your relationships and overall well-being.

CHAPTER THREE

Healing from Past Traumas

I still remember the moment I realized how deeply my past traumas affected my present life. I was at a friend's wedding surrounded by joy and celebration but felt utterly disconnected. The happiness around me seemed like a distant echo, unreachable and foreign. Then, I knew I had to confront the shadows of my past if I ever hoped to embrace my future fully.

Recognizing Trauma

Recognizing trauma is the crucial first step in the healing process. It's not about dwelling on the past but acknowledging its impact on your present. Trauma can leave invisible scars that affect your mental health and relationships in profound ways. Normalizing the experience of trauma is essential. Many people believe they should simply 'get over' their past, but trauma isn't something you can just brush off. It imprints on your psyche, influencing your thoughts, emotions, and behaviors. Understanding this is the first step toward healing. Validating your personal experiences is equally important. Your feelings and reactions are valid, even if others might not understand them. Recognizing and validating your trauma is not about staying stuck in the past but about understanding its impact on your present. It is the first step toward reclaiming your life and building healthier, more fulfilling relationships. Acknowledging your pain and offering yourself compassion creates a foundation for true healing and personal growth.

Trauma can manifest in various forms, each with its unique impact on your life and relationships. Emotional and psychological abuse can be particularly insidious. Unlike physical abuse, which leaves visible marks, emotional and psychological abuse erodes your sense of self-worth and security over time. It might involve constant criticism, manipulation, or control, leaving you feeling powerless and unworthy. Physical abuse is more overt but equally damaging. The fear and pain associated with physical abuse can create deep-seated anxiety and mistrust. Betrayal and infidelity, although different from physical abuse, can also be profoundly traumatic. Discovering that a partner has been unfaithful can shatter your sense of reality and trust, questioning your worth and ability to judge character.

Unresolved trauma often manifests in specific signs and symptoms. Flashbacks and intrusive thoughts are common indicators. You might find yourself reliving traumatic events, unable to escape the memories that haunt you. Seemingly unrelated events can trigger these flashbacks, making everyday life feel unpredictable and unsafe. Emotional numbness and detachment are other signs. To protect yourself from further pain, you might shut down emotionally, distancing yourself from others and even from your feelings. This detachment can make it challenging to connect with others, leaving you feeling isolated and alone. Hypervigilance and anxiety are also common. You might constantly be on edge, always anticipating danger or betrayal. This heightened alertness can be exhausting, affecting your ability to relax and enjoy life.

To begin validating your trauma, consider writing a trauma narrative. This exercise involves writing down your traumatic experiences in detail. It can be a powerful way to externalize your pain, making it more manageable. Start with a specific event and describe it as vividly as possible. Include your thoughts, feelings, and physical sensations. This process can help you gain a clearer understanding of your trauma and its impact on your life. Sharing your experiences in a safe setting can also be incredibly healing. Whether with a trusted friend, family member, or therapist, sharing your story can provide validation and support. It reminds you that you are not alone and that your experiences matter. Practicing self-compassion is another essential exercise. Treat yourself with the kindness and understanding you would offer a friend. When you are self-critical, pause and reframe your thoughts with compassion. Remind yourself that healing is a journey, and taking it one step at a time is okay. Remember, you are not alone in this journey, and self-compassion is a powerful tool in your healing arsenal.

Recognizing and validating your trauma is not about staying stuck in the past but about understanding its impact on your present. It is the first step toward reclaiming your life and building healthier, more fulfilling relationships. Acknowledging your pain and offering yourself compassion creates a foundation for true healing and personal growth. It's important to remember that it's okay to pursue professional help if you feel overwhelmed or if your trauma is affecting your daily life. Therapists and counselors can help you navigate your healing journey.

Processing Emotional Pain through Journaling

Journaling can be a powerful ally in processing emotional pain and facilitating healing. Writing your feelings down creates an emotional outlet that allows you to express yourself freely. Writing offers a safe space for your emotions to flow without judgment and helps you clarify your thoughts and feelings, making them more tangible and easier to understand. As you write, you can see patterns in your emotions and behaviors, helping you gain insights into your inner world. This self-awareness is crucial in healing because it allows you to understand the root causes of your pain and how it impacts your life and relationships. By understanding these root causes, you can begin to address them and move toward healing.

One effective journaling technique for trauma recovery is stream-of-consciousness writing. This method involves writing continuously without worrying about grammar, punctuation, or coherence. Just let your thoughts flow freely onto the paper. Start by setting a timer for 10-15 minutes, and write whatever comes to mind. Don't censor yourself or overthink your words. This practice can help uncover hidden emotions and thoughts you might not know. Another powerful technique is letter writing to your past self or perpetrators. Writing a letter to your younger self can be incredibly healing. Acknowledge the pain and struggles you went through and offer words of comfort and support.

Similarly, writing a letter to someone who hurt you can help you process your feelings. You don't have to send the letter; writing it is what matters. Dialogue journaling with your inner child is another method. This technique involves having a written conversation with your younger self. Ask questions like, "What do you need right now?" or "How can I help you feel safe?" This dialogue can help you reconnect with your inner child and address unresolved emotions.

To guide your journaling practice, consider using specific prompts. These prompts can help you focus your writing and delve deeper into your emotions. For example, "Describe a traumatic event and how it has affected you." This prompt encourages you to reflect on a specific experience and its impact on your life. Another prompt is, "What emotions do you feel when you think about your trauma?" This question helps you identify and name your feelings, a crucial step in processing them. You can also use prompts like, "What do you wish you could tell your younger self about the trauma?" or "How has the trauma affected your relationships?" finally, "What lessons have you learned from your experiences?" This prompt encourages you to find meaning in your pain and recognize the growth from your struggles.

Creating a safe journaling environment is essential for this process to be effective. Choose a private and comfortable space where you can write without interruptions. The place might be a comfy corner in your home or a favorite bench in a park. Setting boundaries around journaling time can also help. Decide on a specific time each day for journaling and stick to it. This routine can provide a sense of structure and stability. Using journaling as a non-judgmental practice is crucial. Allow yourself to write freely without worrying about how it sounds or whether it makes sense. The goal is to express yourself honestly and openly.

Imagine sitting in your favorite chair, a cup of tea by your side and your journal on your lap. You start with a deep breath, then write about a painful memory. As the words flow, you feel a sense of relief, as if a weight is lifted from your shoulders. You write about your anger and sadness; as you do, you understand them better. You realize that these emotions are valid and that it's okay to feel them. This process doesn't magically erase the pain but helps you make sense of it and take a step towards healing.

Guided Visualizations for Trauma Recovery

Guided visualizations are a therapeutic technique that uses imagery to promote healing. This method involves creating vivid images that engage your subconscious mind, helping you process and release emotional pain. Visualizing specific scenarios or symbols fosters a sense of well-being and can reduce stress and anxiety. Guided visualizations can be particularly compelling for individuals dealing with trauma, as they provide a safe space to explore and resolve painful memories without being overwhelmed by them. These visualizations can help you access deeper layers of your psyche, facilitating emotional and mental healing.

One effective guided visualization is creating a safe place. Begin by finding a comfortable spot where you won't be disturbed. Close your eyes and take a few deep breaths to center yourself. Imagine a place where you feel completely safe and at ease. It could be an actual location, a favorite childhood spot, or an imaginary place. Picture every detail vividly—the colors, sounds, and textures. Allow yourself to fully immerse in this safe place, feeling the sense of security and peace it brings. Spend a few minutes here, soaking in the calmness, before gently bringing yourself back to the present moment.

Another powerful visualization is the healing light technique. Start by sitting comfortably and closing your eyes. Take deep breaths to relax your body and mind. Visualize a warm, glowing light above your head. Imagine this light slowly descending, enveloping your entire body. Feel it healing and soothing every part of your being as it moves through you. Picture it dissolving any pain or tension, leaving you with lightness and tranquility. This visualization can help release stored emotional pain, promoting a sense of relief and healing.

Forgiveness visualization is another method that can be transformative. Begin by sitting in a comfortable position and closing your eyes. Take deep breaths to relax. Visualize the person you need to forgive standing in front of you. This person could be someone who hurt you or even yourself. Imagine a soft, warm light surrounding both of you. In your mind, express your feelings and acknowledge the pain caused. Then, visualize yourself letting go of the anger and resentment, allowing the warm light to fill the space between you. This visualization can help you release negative emotions, fostering a sense of forgiveness and peace.

The benefits of guided visualizations are numerous. They can enhance relaxation and calmness by activating the body's natural relaxation response. By engaging the subconscious mind, visualizations can help release stored emotional pain, making it easier to process and move past traumatic experiences. Building a sense of safety and security is another significant benefit. When you consistently practice these visualizations, your mind begins associating them with feelings of peace and safety, making accessing these states in your daily life easier.

Integrating visualizations into your daily routine can maximize their effectiveness. Consider starting your day with a morning visualization. Spend a few minutes visualizing a positive, peaceful day ahead, setting a calm and focused tone. Evening visualizations can help you unwind and prepare for restful sleep. Visualize a safe, comforting place or a healing light before bed to release the day's stresses. During moments of tension, take a quick visualization break. Close your eyes and imagine a calming scenario for a few minutes to regain your composure. Combining visualizations with other mindfulness practices, such as meditation or deep breathing, can enhance their benefits, creating a holistic approach to emotional and mental well-being.

Seeking Professional Help: When and How

Professional help can be a lifeline when dealing with the complexities of trauma recovery. Therapists bring specialized knowledge and skills that can significantly impact your healing process. In this safe and supportive environment, you can explore your feelings and experiences without fear of judgment. This safe space is crucial for delving into painful memories and emotions that might be too overwhelming to confront alone. Therapists are trained to facilitate more profound healing by guiding you through proven techniques and strategies tailored to your needs. They can help uncover underlying issues you may not know, providing insights that can lead to meaningful change.

Recognizing when it's time to seek professional help is vital. Persistent and severe symptoms indicate that you might need additional support. If you find that your anxiety, depression, or emotional distress is not improving despite your best efforts, it may be time to consult a therapist. The inability to function in daily life is another sign. If you struggle to maintain relationships, perform at work, or manage daily tasks, professional help can provide the tools you need to regain control. The lack of progress with self-help methods is also telling. While self-help strategies can be beneficial, they might not be enough for deep-seated trauma. If you're not making the progress you'd hoped for, a therapist can offer more specialized techniques and support.

Finding the right therapist involves several steps. Start by researching different types of therapy to understand which approach might be best for you. Cognitive-behavioral therapy (CBT), Eye Movement Desensitization and Reprocessing (EMDR), and Somatic Experiencing are just a few options. Each has its strengths, and understanding them can help you make an informed choice. Checking credentials and specializations is crucial. Ensure that you have selected a licensed therapist with experience in trauma recovery. Look for reviews or testimonials to gauge their effectiveness. Conducting initial consultations can help you find a good fit. Many therapists offer a first session at a reduced rate or even for free. Use this opportunity to ask questions, discuss your needs, and gauge your comfort level with the therapist. A good therapist is someone you feel comfortable opening up to and understands your unique needs.

Once you start therapy, knowing what to expect can ease some of the initial anxiety. Setting goals and creating a treatment plan is often one of the first steps. Your therapist will work with you to identify specific objectives and outline a plan to achieve them. This collaborative approach aligns your therapy with your personal needs and goals. Building a therapeutic relationship is another essential aspect. Trust and rapport between you and your therapist are crucial for effective treatment. This relationship provides a foundation of safety and support, allowing you to explore your feelings and experiences more deeply. Engaging in therapeutic techniques will be a significant part of your sessions. These might include cognitive restructuring, mindfulness exercises, or trauma-focused techniques like EMDR. Your therapist will guide you through these methods, helping you develop new skills and insights that can lead to healing.

For instance, imagine you're experiencing severe anxiety that disrupts your ability to work and maintain relationships. You've tried various self-help methods, but nothing provides lasting relief. You decide to seek professional help and start by researching therapists who specialize in trauma recovery. After reading reviews and checking credentials, you find a therapist who offers a free initial consultation. During this session, you discuss your symptoms and goals, and the therapist outlines a treatment plan that includes cognitive-behavioral techniques and mindfulness exercises. Over time, the relationship with your therapist becomes a trusted source who helps you develop new strategies for coping and gain insights into the root causes of your anxiety. This professional support provides the structure and guidance you need to make meaningful progress in your healing journey.

Releasing Emotional Baggage

Emotional baggage refers to the unresolved issues and traumas you carry from past experiences into your current life. This baggage can act like an invisible weight, influencing your reactions and interactions in ways you might not fully understand. When you carry unresolved issues, you often project past experiences onto present situations. For instance, if your partner betrayed you in a previous relationship, you might find it hard to trust your current partner, even if they've done nothing to warrant suspicion. This projection creates barriers to intimacy and trust, making building a healthy and fulfilling relationship difficult. Your reactions might frustrate or confuse your partner, leading to misunderstandings and conflicts that further strain the relationship.

Letting go of emotional baggage is crucial for promoting personal growth and building healthier relationship dynamics. Holding onto past traumas is like moving forward while dragging a heavy anchor. Releasing this burden can free you to experience life more fully and openly. It allows you to form connections based on mutual trust and respect rather than fear and suspicion. This process enhances your emotional well-being, giving you the space to heal and grow. It's about creating a clean slate to build new memories and experiences without the shadow of the past looming over you.

One effective strategy for releasing emotional baggage is practicing mindfulness and meditation. These practices help you stay present and grounded, reducing the power of past traumas over your current life. Mindfulness involves paying attention to your thoughts and feelings without judgment. When you notice old patterns or fears creeping in, acknowledge them and gently bring your focus back to the present moment. Meditation can deepen this practice, providing a structured way to calm your mind and release tension. Regular meditation helps create a mental space where you can process and let go of emotional pain, fostering a sense of inner peace.

Cognitive-behavioral techniques can also be highly effective. These methods focus on identifying and challenging negative thought patterns that stem from past traumas. For example, if you think, "I can't trust anyone," challenge this thought by considering evidence to the contrary. Reflect on times when you rewarded trust and others supported you in relationships. By reframing these thoughts, you can break the cycle of negativity and create a more balanced perspective. This shift in thinking can reduce anxiety and improve your ability to form healthy relationships.

Emotional release exercises offer another avenue for letting go of past burdens. Sometimes, the physical act of releasing emotions can be incredibly cathartic. Crying, for instance, can provide a powerful outlet for pent-up sadness and grief. Find a safe space where you can let your emotions flow without inhibition. Shouting or expressing anger in a controlled environment, like on a pillow or during a workout, can also help release frustration and rage. These exercises allow you to physically and emotionally release the weight of past traumas, creating space for healing and new experiences.

Consider Frank, a 40-year-old architect. He tensed as his girlfriend Tara asked if he wanted to meet her parents. Memories of his ex's constant criticism flooded back, triggering anger and fear. He rushed out, leaving a confused Tara behind.

Realizing he needed change, Frank sought help. He started with a mindfulness app, learning to observe his thoughts without getting caught up in them. During one session, he visualized his anger as a fire and watched it slowly die down, understanding that his emotions didn't have to control him.

Frank also began cognitive-behavioral therapy, identifying negative thought patterns from his past relationship. He learned to challenge these thoughts, like when Tara complimented his work and he initially doubted her sincerity.

A breakthrough came when Frank allowed himself to cry during a therapy session, releasing years of pent-up emotion. Sharing this vulnerability with Tara deepened their connection.

Over months of practice and therapy, Frank's anger subsided. He became more present with Tara, appreciating her love without constant fear. Six months later, as they stood on her parents' porch, Frank felt anxious but no longer overwhelmed. He was learning to trust and love again, proving to himself that he could build the relationship he had always wanted.

Kristin, a 33-year-old marketing executive, stared at her boyfriend Paul's social media post with his attractive coworker. Her heart raced, as she had her usual thoughts that he was going to cheat on her. Two years earlier, Kristin had discovered her ex-fiancé's affair, leaving deep scars.

Recognizing that her baseless suspicions threatened to unravel her romance, Kristin took decisive action. She began by downloading a meditation app, dedicating time each day to practice awareness of her worried thoughts without becoming entangled in them. Simultaneously, Kristin initiated counseling sessions, where she delved into cognitive restructuring methods to confront and reshape her pessimistic beliefs.

Kristin's therapist suggested writing an unsent letter to her ex-fiancé to release lingering pain. After reading it aloud, she burned it, symbolically letting go of her past hurt.

Kristin was challenged when Paul attended an out-of-town conference. Instead of panicking, Kristin used her new tools to manage her anxiety. She meditated, challenged negative thoughts, and journaled her feelings.

Over time, Kristin's fears faded. She learned to trust not just Paul, but herself, building a relationship based on genuine connection rather than fear.

Rebuilding Trust After Betrayal

Rebuilding trust after betrayal is like repairing a shattered vase. The process starts with acknowledging the betrayal. First, you must confront the reality of what happened—facing the pain and disappointment head-on rather than sweeping it under the rug. Open and honest communication is crucial here. Both partners must be willing to discuss the betrayal openly, sharing their feelings and perspectives. This dialogue helps clear the air, allowing you to understand each other's pain and intentions. Setting realistic expectations is also essential. Rebuilding trust is not a quick fix; it takes time and consistent effort. Both partners need to agree on steps to restore trust and what success will look like.

Trusting yourself is a fundamental part of the healing process. After betrayal, you may lose confidence in your judgment. You might question your ability to make good decisions or to trust your instincts. Rebuilding self-trust involves acknowledging that you made the best decisions you could with the information you had at the time. It's about giving yourself grace and recognizing that everyone makes mistakes. Building self-confidence is another crucial element.

Engage in activities that make you feel good about yourself and remind you of your strengths. Practicing self-care is essential during this time. Taking care of your physical, emotional, and mental well-being can bolster your confidence and resilience, helping you navigate the healing process more effectively.

Rebuilding trust in relationships requires concrete actions. Establishing clear boundaries is a crucial step. These boundaries act as guidelines for acceptable behavior and help create a sense of safety and respect. Both partners must agree on these boundaries and commit to honoring them. Consistent and reliable actions are necessary to rebuild trust. Meaning following through on promises, being dependable, and demonstrating your commitment to change over time. Actions speak louder than words. Consistency is critical to proving that the betrayal will not happen again. Seeking couples therapy can also be beneficial. A therapist can provide a neutral space for both partners to express their feelings and work through the betrayal. Therapy can offer tools and techniques to rebuild trust and improve communication, making the healing process more structured and supported.

Here is the case of Lily and Sam. The text message on Lily's phone confirmed her worst fears: Sam, her husband of eight years, was having an affair. Confronting him led to hours of tears, anger, and pain.

In the weeks that followed, Lily struggled with rage and despair, while Sam, consumed by guilt, slept on the couch. Surprisingly, it was Lily who suggested couples therapy.

Their first session with the therapist was tense. Over time, they explored the roots of the affair. Sam admitted feeling unseen in their marriage, which resonated with Lily.

Their therapist introduced "affair-proofing" techniques, including setting boundaries and improving emotional communication. A pivotal exercise involved writing letters to each other, expressing pain, remorse, and commitment to change.

Outside therapy, Sam worked to rebuild trust through consistent actions, while Lily focused on her self-esteem, returning to painting and joining a support group.

Six months later, they faced a major test when Sam attended a work event where his former affair partner was present. They prepared together, and Lily managed her fears without spiraling.

A year after the affair, as they cooked dinner together, Lily realized they were stronger than before. Sam agreed, expressing gratitude for Lily's willingness to fight for their relationship.

Their journey of healing was ongoing, but they faced it together with newfound strength and hope, having transformed their relationship through the pain of betrayal.

Another example is Kimberly, 43. Six months ago, she'd have laughed at the idea of painting, but now it was a valuable tool in rebuilding her shattered self-confidence.

Eight months earlier, she'd discovered flirtatious messages between Tom, her partner, and his coworker. This betrayal had shaken Kimberly's trust in herself, leading to constant self-doubt in all aspects of her life.

One evening, a quote caught her eye: "The most important relationship you'll ever have is with yourself." Realizing she'd forgotten to trust herself, Kimberly took action. She joined an art class, started journaling daily decisions, and reconnected with an old friend.

A solo weekend trip to the coast marked a turning point. For the first time in months, Kimberly felt at peace, having planned and enjoyed the trip on her own.

Back home, Kimberly found herself more self-assured in all areas of her life, like standing up to her overbearing boss for the first time. "I believe my project timeline is realistic," she said firmly in a team meeting, surprising herself with her confidence. Her boss, taken aback, actually listened and agreed.

The real test came when Tom reached out, asking to meet and talk. In the past, Kimberly would have agonized over the decision, seeking advice from everyone she knew. This time, she tuned into her feelings and firmly declined. She realized she trusted herself to know what was best for her own well-being

As Kimberly painted she reflected on her journey. Each small step had brought her closer to becoming a strong, confident woman, with newfound self-assurance and hope. Kimberly realized this trust in herself was the foundation she needed for all future relationships.

Rebuilding trust after betrayal is challenging but transformative. It involves honest communication, setting boundaries, and consistent actions. Trusting yourself is equally important, as it lays the foundation for trusting others. With time, effort, and the proper support, it's possible to rebuild trust and create a stronger, more resilient relationship. This journey of healing and growth paves the way for deeper connections and a more fulfilling life.

Chapter 3 has guided you through recognizing and validating trauma, processing emotional pain through journaling, using guided visualizations, seeking professional help, releasing emotional baggage, and rebuilding trust after betrayal. These steps form a comprehensive path toward healing. As you progress, you'll learn how to build self-esteem and confidence, essential components for sustaining emotional growth and healthy relationships, which we will explore in the next chapter.

CHAPTER FOUR

Managing Social Anxiety in Romantic Contexts

I remember sitting across from someone on a first date, my mind racing about what to say next, how to act, and whether or not they were judging me. My palms were sweaty, and I felt a tightening in my chest, making it hard to breathe. Social anxiety had a firm grip on me, turning what should have been an enjoyable evening into a nerve-wracking ordeal. If this sounds familiar, you are not alone. Social anxiety in romantic contexts is a common struggle and can profoundly impact your dating life.

Understanding Social Anxiety and Its Impact on Dating

Social anxiety is a pervasive fear of being judged or scrutinized by others. It manifests uniquely in dating situations, often turning what should be moments of connection and enjoyment into episodes of intense fear and discomfort. Fear of judgment during dates can be particularly crippling. You might obsess over every word and action, terrified that you'll say something wrong or be perceived negatively. This fear can overshadow the entire date, making it hard to be present and genuine. Avoidance of social gatherings is another common manifestation. The prospect of meeting new people or being in a crowded place can be overwhelming, leading you to decline invitations and miss out on opportunities to connect. Overanalyzing interactions post-date is also typical. After the date, you might replay conversations in your head, scrutinizing every detail for signs of disapproval or mistakes you think you made. This constant analysis can keep you trapped in a cycle of self-doubt and anxiety.

Social anxiety takes a significant toll on your emotional and psychological well-being. Increased stress levels are almost inevitable. The constant worry about how you are perceived and the fear of making mistakes can keep your body in a heightened state of stress, affecting your overall health. Lowered self-esteem often accompanies social anxiety. When you continuously worry about being judged, it's easy to start believing something is inherently wrong with you. This negative self-perception can erode your confidence and make it even more challenging to engage in social situations. Feelings of isolation are also common. Social anxiety can make you withdraw from social interactions, leading to loneliness and a sense of disconnection from others.

Several common triggers can exacerbate social anxiety in romantic contexts. Fear of rejection is a significant one. The possibility of someone not reciprocating your feelings or interest can be terrifying, making you hesitant to put yourself out there. Meeting new people is another trigger. The unknowns of a new person's personality, interests, and perceptions can create a sense of unpredictability that fuels anxiety. Uncertainty in relationship status can also be a trigger. When unsure where you stand with someone, it can lead to constant second-guessing and overanalyzing their actions and words.

The long-term impact of unmanaged social anxiety on relationships can be profound. Difficulty in forming and maintaining relationships is one of the most significant consequences. The fear and avoidance behaviors associated with social anxiety can make it hard to initiate and sustain romantic connections. Strained communication is another issue. When you are anxious, it can be challenging to communicate openly and effectively, leading to misunderstandings and conflicts. Emotional distance can also develop. The constant worry and fear can create a barrier to emotional intimacy, making it hard to connect on a deeper level with your partner.

Reflection Exercise: Identifying Your Triggers

Take a few moments to reflect on your experiences with social anxiety in dating. Write down specific situations that triggered your anxiety. Consider what aspects of these situations were most challenging for you. Reflecting on your triggers can help you understand and manage your social anxiety more effectively.

Gradual Exposure Exercises for Dating Confidence

Gradual exposure is a technique for incrementally facing anxiety-provoking situations. This method helps build confidence by allowing you to confront your fears in manageable steps. The idea is to start with low-stress scenarios and gradually move to more challenging ones. Doing this can build tolerance and reduce the fear associated with these situations over time. It's like slowly dipping your toes into cold water before fully diving in. This approach helps you acclimate to the discomfort, making it less overwhelming each time you face it.

To begin with, start with low-stress scenarios. Texting someone new can be an excellent initial step. It allows you to engage in social interaction without the immediate pressure of face-to-face communication. Focus on casual, low-stakes conversations. You might text a friend of a friend or join an online community where you can practice socializing. As you become more comfortable, progress to moderate-stress scenarios. Short coffee dates are an excellent next step. These settings are typically less formal and offer a relaxed environment for conversation. The duration is shorter, making it easier to manage any anxiety that arises. Finally, advance to high-stress scenarios like attending social events with a date. These situations involve more people and potential for interaction, but by this stage, you'll have built a level of comfort and confidence to help you navigate them more smoothly.

The benefits of gradual exposure for managing social anxiety are substantial. First, it reduces fear and anxiety by allowing you to face your fears in a controlled and incremental way. Each successful interaction reinforces the idea that you can handle these situations, diminishing your anxiety's power over time. Improved self-confidence is another significant benefit. As you navigate these scenarios successfully, your belief in your ability to handle social interactions grows. This newfound confidence can spill over into other areas of your life, enhancing your overall self-esteem. Enhanced social skills are also a byproduct of gradual exposure. The more you practice, the better you read social cues, engage in conversation, and manage social interactions effectively.

Consider the story of Jane, 28. Jane, stared at her phone, hesitating to create a dating app profile. Social anxiety had plagued her since high school, causing her to miss out on many social experiences. Inspired by her sister's wedding video, Jane decided to take action.

Instead of jumping into dating, Jane joined an online community for people with social anxiety. Her first post received supportive responses, making her feel understood. Over weeks, she built confidence through text-based interactions.

Two months later, Jane met Maya, a community member, for coffee. Despite initial nervousness, Jane relaxed as they bonded over shared experiences. Encouraged, she set a goal of weekly meetups with different community members.

Four months into her journey, Jane created her dating app profile. Her first match suggested an art gallery, but Jane compromised with a park walk followed by coffee. During the date with Michael, Jane applied her practiced conversation skills, surprising herself by enjoying the experience.

As Jane recounted the date to her online community, she realized how far she'd come. Through gradual exposure – from online interactions to in-person meetups to dating – she had expanded her comfort zone. While anxiety wasn't gone, Jane had developed tools to manage it, opening up new social and romantic possibilities.

Christopher, 32, nervously prepared for his first dinner party in years, a constant reminder of his social anxiety. After years of avoiding social gatherings, Christopher decided to face his fears with help from his therapist who suggested a gradual exposure plan.

They started small, with Christopher inviting his best friend over for pizza and a movie. Using breathing techniques, Christopher managed his anxiety and enjoyed the evening. Encouraged, he progressed to a small gathering at his friend's place, then joined a book club and initiated lunch outings with coworkers.

Each experience built Christopher's confidence. He learned to handle more than he thought possible, developing coping strategies for various social situations.

At Jen's dinner party, Christopher felt both anxious and excited. When conversation lulled, he shared a funny work story, surprising himself. As the night progressed, he genuinely enjoyed the interactions and even stayed to help clean up.

Driving home, Christopher reflected on his journey. While anxiety wasn't gone, it no longer controlled him. Each gradual step had transformed social interactions from sources of dread to opportunities for joy.

Christopher's life had become fuller and more connected through this process of gradual exposure, opening up a world of possibilities he once thought impossible.

Gradual exposure exercises offer a structured and effective way to manage social anxiety in dating contexts. By starting with low-stress scenarios and gradually progressing to more challenging ones, you can build confidence, reduce fear, and enhance social skills. Like those of Jane and Christopher, real-life examples demonstrate how this technique can transform your approach to social interactions, making dating a more enjoyable and less anxiety-ridden experience.

Coping Strategies for Anxiety in Social Situations

When you experience social anxiety, having a toolkit of coping strategies can make all the difference. Deep breathing exercises are a straightforward yet effective way to manage stress. Begin by finding a quiet spot where you can sit comfortably. Inhale deeply through your nose, allowing your abdomen to expand fully. Hold your breath for a count of four, then exhale slowly through your mouth. This simple controlled breathing can help calm your nervous system and bring you back to the present moment.

Grounding techniques are another valuable tool in your anxiety management arsenal. These techniques involve focusing on sensory details to anchor yourself in the present. One effective method is the 5-4-3-2-1 exercise. Start by identifying five things you can see around you. Next, focus on four things you can touch: the texture of your clothing or the surface of a nearby object. Then, identify three things you can hear, like the hum of a fan or distant chatter. Follow this by noticing two things you can smell and one thing you can taste. This exercise helps divert your mind from anxious thoughts and returns your focus to the present.

Positive visualization is another powerful coping strategy. It involves imagining a successful social interaction before it happens. Find a quiet place and close your eyes. Picture yourself in the social situation you are anxious about. Visualize everything in detail: the setting, the people, and the conversation. Imagine feeling confident and at ease, handling the interaction smoothly and successfully. This mental rehearsal can help reduce anxiety and build confidence, making navigating the situation more manageable.

Preparing your coping strategies in advance is crucial for managing social anxiety effectively. Create a mental toolkit of methods that you can draw upon when needed. Practice these techniques regularly in low-stress environments to build your confidence. Rehearsing them beforehand ensures that you are familiar with the methods and can employ them seamlessly when anxiety strikes. For example, deep breathing exercises should be practiced daily to become second nature. Use grounding techniques to reinforce their effectiveness during routine activities, like waiting in line or sitting in traffic. Visualize positive outcomes for various scenarios, not just social interactions, to build a habit of positive thinking.

When it comes to using coping strategies during dates, discretion is critical. If you feel overwhelmed, take a break to breathe and regroup. Excuse yourself to the restroom or step outside for a moment. Use this time to practice deep breathing exercises to calm yourself before rejoining the date. Incorporate grounding objects into your routine. Carry a small, discreet item like a stress ball or smooth stone in your pocket. When anxious, discreetly touch or hold the object to ground yourself. This tactile sensation can help anchor you in the present and reduce anxiety.

Visualizing positive outcomes before entering a venue can also set a positive tone for your date. Take a few moments to close your eyes and imagine the date going well. Picture yourself engaging in pleasant conversation, feeling relaxed and confident. This mental rehearsal can boost your mood and reduce pre-date jitters. Remember, it's okay to use these strategies discreetly during the date. If you feel anxious, take a deep breath, focus on your grounding object, and remind yourself of the positive visualization you practiced earlier.

Incorporating these coping strategies into your routine can make a significant difference in managing social anxiety. Whether preparing for a date or navigating a social event, these tools can help you stay calm, present, and confident. With practice and preparation, you can reduce the impact of social anxiety and enjoy more fulfilling social interactions.

Role-Playing Scenarios to Practice Social Skills

Role-playing can be an incredibly effective method for developing social skills. It provides a safe space to practice interactions without the pressure of real-world consequences. This controlled environment allows you to experiment with different approaches, receive feedback, and make adjustments, helping you build confidence over time. Repetition is critical in reducing anxiety, and role-playing allows you to practice repeatedly until the skills become more natural. Each session builds on the last, gradually making social interactions less intimidating. Knowing you have a supportive space to practice can make real-life situations more manageable.

Consider role-playing scenarios that mirror everyday social interactions. Initiating a conversation with a stranger is a fundamental skill. Start by practicing with a trusted friend or therapist. Imagine you're at a social event and need to introduce yourself. Practice your opening lines, how you'll maintain eye contact, and what follow-up questions you might ask to keep the conversation flowing. Another valuable scenario involves handling awkward silences during a date. These moments can feel excruciating, but practicing how to navigate them can reduce your anxiety. Work on having a few go-to topics or questions ready to fill the gaps. Responding to compliments and criticism is also crucial. Practice accepting compliments graciously without deflecting or downplaying them. Similarly, practice how to respond to criticism constructively without becoming defensive.

Partnering with a trusted friend or therapist is essential for effective role-playing. Choose someone who understands your goals and can provide constructive feedback. Setting realistic and achievable goals for each session can keep you focused and motivated. For example, aim to initiate a conversation without feeling the need to rush through it or practice maintaining eye contact for a specific duration. After each role-playing exercise, debrief with your partner. Discuss what went well and identify areas for improvement. This feedback loop helps you refine your skills and build confidence.

Incorporate role-playing into your regular practice with a few strategies. Schedule regular sessions to ensure consistency. Consistency is crucial for building and maintaining new skills. Start with more straightforward scenarios and gradually increase the complexity. For instance, begin practicing small talk and progress to more challenging interactions, like navigating a disagreement. Keeping a progress journal can be immensely helpful. Document each session, noting what you practiced, what went well, and what you found challenging. Reflecting on your progress can provide motivation and highlight areas that need more focus.

Imagine working with a friend who acts as a stranger at a party. You practice introducing yourself, asking open-ended questions, and maintaining the flow of conversation. Your friend provided feedback, noting that you seemed relaxed and engaged but occasionally looked away when you felt nervous. Take this feedback and focus on maintaining eye contact in your next session. Over time, you notice that initiating conversations becomes less daunting, and you feel more comfortable engaging with new people. This gradual improvement shows the power of role-playing in building social confidence.

Another scenario might involve practicing how to handle a compliment. Your friend compliments your appearance or a recent achievement, and you practice responding with a simple "Thank you" rather than deflecting or downplaying the compliment. This exercise helps you become more comfortable accepting positive feedback, which can boost your self-esteem. Over time, these skills become second nature, making real-life interactions smoother and less anxiety-inducing.

Building Emotional Resilience in Social Contexts

Emotional resilience is adapting to stress and adversity while maintaining emotional stability. It's about bouncing back from setbacks and handling difficult situations with grace. Emotional resilience is crucial for managing social anxiety and building healthy relationships in social interactions. When you develop this resilience, you can navigate the ups and downs of social encounters more effectively. It allows you to stay calm under pressure, think clearly during challenging moments, and respond thoughtfully rather than react impulsively. This stability is the foundation for positive social interactions and meaningful connections.

Developing emotional resilience offers numerous benefits. One of the most significant is better stress management. With resilience, you can handle stress more effectively, reducing its impact on your mental and physical health. This improved stress management translates to increased confidence. When you trust your ability to cope with challenges, you approach social situations with assurance. This confidence can make you more engaging and approachable, enhancing social interactions. Additionally, emotional resilience enhances problem-solving skills. When faced with social challenges, resilient individuals can think creatively and find practical solutions, improving their ability to navigate complex social dynamics.

Building emotional resilience involves several actionable steps. Practicing mindfulness and meditation is a powerful way to enhance resilience. These practices help you stay present and centered, reducing the impact of stress and anxiety. Start with simple mindfulness exercises, like focusing on your breath or observing your thoughts without judgment. Gradually incorporate meditation into your routine, dedicating a few minutes daily to this practice. Engaging in regular physical exercise is another effective strategy. Exercise releases endorphins, which improve mood and reduce stress. Find an activity you enjoy, whether jogging, yoga, or dancing, and make it a regular part of your routine. Developing a solid support network is also crucial. Surround yourself with people who understand and support you. These connections provide emotional safety and encouragement, helping you build resilience through positive relationships.

Emma, 29, stood nervously in her first public yoga class, a significant step for someone with crippling social anxiety resulting from past failed relationships. After a panic attack at her friend's baby shower, Emma decided to build her emotional resilience.

She started with daily breathing exercises and then joined a yoga class as a mindfulness practice. Initially anxious, Emma found support from fellow students and gradually improved.

As her physical strength grew, Emma noticed changes in her mental state. The breathing techniques helped her manage anxiety in other areas of life. She began accepting lunch invitations and joined a book club, pushing herself to engage socially.

Six months later, Emma attended her company's annual gala, an event she'd avoided for years. Though anxiety still ebbed and flowed, she experienced moments of genuine connection.

Emma realized that while anxiety hadn't disappeared, it no longer controlled her. She had developed resilience to face social situations and find joy in connections. Each small step - from breathing exercises to yoga to work events - had rebuilt her emotional strength.

Drew, a 39-year-old copywriter, with severe social anxiety, moved to Chicago and after three months the city felt like a nightmare of unfamiliar faces. Social anxiety kept him isolated, declining invitations and retreating from potential connections.

Drew knew he had to make changes so he did some research to find the tools to help. He used to be an avid runner, so he got out his old running shoes and hit the lakeshore path. The first run was tough, but he was determined to stick with it.

Running became a daily habit. During one run, a brief chat with another jogger boosted Drew's confidence. He joined a hiking group on Meetup.com, facing his fears with newly learned breathing techniques.

The hike challenged Drew, but nature's beauty grounded him. He managed several conversations and even exchanged numbers with a fellow writer.

Encouraged, Drew expanded his social circle. He joined a weekly board game night and started accepting lunch invitations at work. Progress was slow but steady.

Six months later, Drew attended a networking event for writers. His anxiety ebbed and flowed, but he engaged in meaningful conversations and exchanged business cards.

It is still a constant effort, but anxiety no longer controlled him. Through exercise, mindfulness, and gradual exposure, he'd built resilience he never knew he possessed.

Chicago was transforming from a place of isolation to one of opportunity. Drew's journey continued, but he now faced the future with excitement, rediscovering himself and embracing a more confident version of who he could be.

Managing Anxiety Before and During Dates

Preparation can be your best ally in managing pre-date anxiety. Planning the date details can significantly reduce uncertainty, a common trigger for anxiety. Knowing where you're going, what you'll be doing, and what you'll wear can provide a sense of control and confidence. Visualization is another powerful tool. Spend a few moments imagining the date going well. Picture yourself feeling calm, engaged in pleasant conversation, and enjoying the experience. This positive mental rehearsal can make the actual date more optimistic. Practicing relaxation techniques before the date can also make a big difference. Activities like yoga, meditation, or a warm bath can help calm your nerves and create a sense of peace before stepping out.

To manage pre-date anxiety effectively, employ specific techniques. Deep breathing exercises are a simple yet effective method. Find a quiet space, sit comfortably, and take a deep breath through your nose, allowing your abdomen to expand.

Hold it for a count of four, then exhale slowly through your mouth. Repeat this process several times to help calm your nervous system. Positive affirmations can also be constructive. Remind yourself of your strengths and positive qualities. Phrases like "I am confident and capable" or "I am worthy of love and respect" can bolster your self-esteem and reduce anxiety. Physical exercise is another excellent way to release tension. A short run, a workout session, or even a brisk walk can help burn off nervous energy and leave you feeling more relaxed.

During the date, staying calm and present is crucial. Focused breathing techniques can be a lifesaver. If you feel anxiety creeping in, take a few deep breaths to center yourself. This simple act can help you regain control and stay grounded. Grounding exercises are also practical at the moment. You might carry a small, discreet object like a smooth stone or stress ball in your pocket. When you start to feel anxious, touch or hold the object to help you stay present. This tactile sensation can anchor you and reduce feelings of anxiety. Active listening can also help keep your mind from wandering into anxious thoughts. Focus on what your date is saying, ask open-ended questions, and show genuine interest, which enables you to stay present and fosters a deeper connection with your date.

Real-life examples can illustrate how these strategies work in practice. Take this anecdote from Natalie. She was getting ready for a date and her stomach was in a knot of anxiety. At 34, she'd been on countless first dates, but each one felt like a monumental challenge. Tonight's date with David, a charming software engineer she'd met online, was no exception.

But this time, Natalie was determined to break her cycle of pre-date panic. She'd been working with her therapist on anxiety management techniques, and tonight was the night to put them into practice.

Taking a deep breath, Natalie began her new pre-date ritual. She closed her eyes and visualized the evening ahead, imagining herself laughing and chatting comfortably with David. "I am worthy of connection," she whispered, the first of several positive affirmations she'd prepared.

Natalie had meticulously planned every detail of her outfit, choosing clothes that made her feel confident and comfortable. She'd even visited the restaurant earlier in the week, familiarizing herself with the ambiance and menu to reduce unknowns.

As she left her apartment, Natalie slipped a small, smooth stone into her pocket – a grounding object her therapist had suggested. Feeling its cool surface helped anchor her to the present moment when anxiety threatened to spiral.

At the restaurant, Natalie's heart raced as she spotted David. Instinctively, her hand found the stone in her pocket. She took three deep breaths, counting slowly as she'd practiced.

To her surprise, the conversation flowed easily. Natalie found herself genuinely listening to David's stories, asking follow-up questions instead of frantically planning what to say next. When a moment of awkward silence fell, instead of panicking, Natalie simply smiled and took a sip of water, remembering her therapist's advice that pauses were natural.

As the evening progressed, Natalie realized something remarkable – she was actually enjoying herself. The anxiety that usually clouded her mind on dates had receded to a manageable hum.

After the night ended, Natalie felt a surge of pride. Her date with David had been pleasant, but the real victory was personal. Through preparation, mindfulness, and self-compassion, she'd navigated a typically stressful situation with newfound ease. Natalie knew that managing her anxiety would be an ongoing process, but tonight had shown her what was possible. For the first time in years, she felt hopeful about dating – and about herself.

Managing anxiety before and during dates involves a combination of preparation, specific techniques, and strategies to stay present. By planning the details, practicing relaxation methods, and using tools like deep breathing, positive affirmations, and grounding exercises, you can significantly reduce anxiety and enjoy your dating experiences more fully. Real-life examples, like those of Natalie, demonstrate how to implement these strategies effectively, leading to more successful and enjoyable dates.

Dear Reader,

Thank you for joining me on this journey of emotional growth and self-discovery. Your courage in facing relationship anxiety and overthinking is truly inspiring. As we progress in this book, I have a heartfelt request: if my words have touched you, helped you, or sparked a change in your life, would you consider sharing your experience with others in the form of a review on Amazon?

Your review can be a beacon of hope for someone struggling with similar challenges. It only takes a few minutes, but its impact can be profound. Your honest thoughts can guide others to find the support they need.

Every review is a step towards building a community of understanding and healing. Thank you for your time, your trust, and for being part of this transformative journey.

With gratitude,

Cynthia Shepherd

Scan the QR code above with the camera on your phone or tap here:
https://www.amazon.com/review/
review-your-purchases/?asin=B0DJ2WPR3J

CHAPTER FIVE

Developing Secure Attachment Styles

It's a quiet Sunday afternoon, and you're snuggled on your couch with a cup of tea. Glancing through your phone, you notice a picture of a happy couple effortlessly smiling and holding hands. A pang of longing hits you. It's not just the desire for a relationship that strikes you but the yearning for a secure, unwavering connection. You wonder, "Why do I always feel so anxious or distant in my relationships?" This chapter will help you uncover the roots of your attachment style and guide you toward more secure, fulfilling connections.

Self-Assessments to Identify Your Attachment Style

Understanding your attachment style is crucial for navigating relationship anxiety and overthinking. Self-assessment is your first step toward gaining self-awareness, identifying relational patterns, and setting the stage for personal growth.

Knowing your attachment style gives you insights into why you react the way you do in relationships. This awareness can help you break free from unhealthy patterns and build stronger, more secure connections.

Attachment styles are the emotional bonds we form with others, and they stem from our earliest interactions with caregivers. There are four main attachment styles: secure, anxious, avoidant, and disorganized. A secure attachment style develops when caregivers consistently respond to a child's needs. As an adult, you can trust others easily, communicate openly, and feel comfortable with intimacy. Anxious attachment, on the other hand, arises from inconsistent caregiving. If you have this style, you might crave closeness but constantly worry about your partner's commitment, seeking constant reassurance and fearing abandonment.

Avoidant attachment forms when caregivers are emotionally unavailable. If this is your style, you might value independence to the point of avoiding emotional closeness. You may need help to rely on others and often prefer to keep a distance. Disorganized attachment results from caregivers who are both a source of comfort and fear, often due to abusive or neglectful behavior. This style features erratic and unpredictable behaviors in relationships, where you might oscillate between seeking closeness and pushing others away.

To help you identify your attachment style, let's dive into a comprehensive self-assessment quiz. This quiz consists of multiple-choice questions related to your relationship behaviors. Answer each question honestly to gain the most accurate insights.

Attachment Style Quiz:

How do you feel when your partner doesn't respond to your messages immediately?

A) I trust they are busy and will reply when they can.

B) I feel anxious and wonder if they are upset with me.

C) I feel relieved because I need my space.

D) I feel a mix of anxiety and anger, unsure of how to react.

How do you usually react during conflicts with your partner?

A) I stay calm and discuss the issue openly.

B) I become anxious and need reassurance.

C) I withdraw and avoid the conflict.

D) I have intense emotional reactions and feel confused.

How comfortable are you with expressing your needs to your partner?

A) Very comfortable; open communication is essential.

B) Somewhat comfortable, I worry about how they will react.

C) Uncomfortable; I prefer to handle things on my own.

D) Extremely uncomfortable; I feel overwhelmed and unsure.

What is your biggest fear in a relationship?

A) Losing the connection due to external factors.

B) Being abandoned or rejected.

C) Being suffocated or losing my independence.

D) Being hurt or betrayed again.

Scoring Guide:
Mostly A's: Secure Attachment
Mostly B's: Anxious Attachment
Mostly C's: Avoidant Attachment
Mostly D's: Disorganized Attachment

Each attachment style has its strengths and challenges. If you have a secure attachment, you likely experience healthy communication and trust in your relationships. You can express your needs and emotions openly and trust your partner to do the same. Anxious attachment brings a deep desire for closeness and connection, but it also comes with fears of abandonment and a need for constant reassurance. This can lead to behaviors that strain the relationship, such as clinginess or overanalyzing your partner's actions.

Avoidant attachment offers the strength of independence and self-reliance but can make emotional intimacy challenging. You might struggle to open up and connect deeply with your partner, leading to feelings of loneliness and isolation. Disorganized attachment combines the need for closeness with a fear of it, resulting in unpredictable and erratic behaviors. You might find yourself in a constant state of emotional turmoil, unsure of how to balance your need for connection with your fear of getting hurt.

Understanding your attachment style is the first step toward creating healthier relationships. By recognizing your patterns and behaviors, you can make conscious changes that lead to more secure and fulfilling connections. Whether you have a safe, anxious, avoidant, or disorganized attachment style, the key is to approach your relationships with awareness, compassion, and a willingness to grow.

Moving from Anxious to Secure Attachment

Anxious attachment often feels like an emotional roller-coaster. You might constantly fear abandonment, which leads to behaviors that seek constant reassurance from your partner. This fear stems from a deep-seated belief that you are not enough and your partner will leave if you aren't perfect. You may overanalyze their every word and action, searching for signs of impending rejection. This creates a cycle of anxiety and neediness that can strain your relationship. Trust becomes a significant hurdle, as the slightest delay in a text message or a change in tone can send you spiraling into doubt and fear.

Transitioning from an anxious attachment style to a secure one requires building self-confidence and self-worth. Start by recognizing your intrinsic value. You are worthy of love and respect, not because of what you do but because of who you are. Engage in activities that make you feel good about yourself. This could be pursuing a hobby, setting and achieving small goals, or surrounding yourself with supportive people. Practicing emotional regulation techniques can also help. When you feel anxiety creeping in, take a moment to breathe deeply and ground yourself. Remind yourself that not every thought is a fact. Enhancing communication skills is another crucial step. Learn to express your needs and feelings openly without demanding reassurance. Use "I" statements to communicate your emotions without blaming your partner.

Specific exercises can be incredibly helpful in managing anxious behaviors in relationships. Mindfulness meditation is a powerful tool for calming the mind and reducing anxiety. Spend a few minutes each day focusing on your breath, letting go of intrusive thoughts as they arise. This practice helps you stay present and reduces the tendency to overthink. Journaling is another effective method. Write down your anxious thoughts and challenge them. Ask yourself whether concrete evidence supports these fears or if irrational beliefs fuel them. This process can help you gain a clearer perspective and reduce anxiety. Visualization exercises can also promote calmness. Imagine a peaceful scene, like a serene beach or a quiet forest. Visualize yourself feeling secure and loved in your relationship. This mental imagery can create a sense of peace and stability.

Consider Jessica, who struggled with anxious attachment for years. She constantly needed reassurance from her partner, which led to frequent conflicts. Jessica decided to take control of her anxiety by practicing mindfulness meditation daily. She also began journaling her thoughts, challenging the irrational ones. Jessica noticed a significant reduction in her anxiety over time. She felt more secure in her relationship and could communicate her needs without fear.

Another example is Peter, who attended therapy sessions to address his anxious attachment. Through therapy, he learned to build self-worth and practice emotional regulation techniques. Peter started to see himself as deserving of love and respect, which transformed his interactions with his partner. He no longer felt the need to seek constant reassurance, and his relationship flourished as a result.

Moving from anxious to secure attachment is a gradual process that requires patience and perseverance. But with the right strategies and consistent effort, you can develop a more secure and fulfilling relationship.

Overcoming Avoidant Attachment Behaviors

Avoidant attachment can be a subtle yet powerful force in your relationships. If you have an avoidant attachment style, you likely exhibit emotional distancing, a reluctance to commit, and a tendency to suppress your emotions. Opening up to your partner or relying on them for emotional support may be challenging. Instead, you prefer to keep a safe distance, managing your feelings alone. This self-reliance might seem a strength but can create barriers to deep emotional intimacy. You may be reluctant to commit fully, fearing that doing so will compromise your independence or lead to vulnerability. Suppressing emotions is another hallmark of avoidant attachment. You might downplay your feelings or avoid discussing them altogether, making building a genuine connection with your partner complex.

Addressing avoidant attachment behaviors is no easy feat. The fear of vulnerability can be overwhelming. Opening up emotionally is like exposing a raw nerve, making you susceptible to rejection or hurt. Breaking long-standing habits of emotional distance and self-reliance requires purposeful effort and a willingness to step out of your comfort zone. Developing emotional intimacy can feel foreign and uncomfortable, but it's crucial to building healthier relationships. The challenge lies in balancing independence and being emotionally available to your partner.

To build emotional intimacy, start with gradual self-disclosure. Share details about your life, feelings, and experiences with your partner. This progressive sharing helps build trust and comfort over time. Practicing empathy and active listening can also strengthen your emotional connection. Listen attentively and respond compassionately when your partner shares their thoughts and feelings. Show that you understand and care about their experiences. Engaging in shared activities can further enhance intimacy. Participate in activities you both enjoy, whether cooking together, hiking, or watching a movie. These shared experiences create positive memories and foster a sense of togetherness.

To reduce avoidance behaviors, consider journaling about your fears of intimacy. Write about what makes you hesitant to open up and explore the root causes of these fears. Reflecting on your thoughts can provide insights and help you understand your avoidance patterns. Setting small, achievable goals for emotional openness can also be beneficial. Start with minor steps, like expressing a simple feeling or sharing a personal story. Gradually increase the level of emotional disclosure as you become more comfortable. Mindfulness practices help you stay present in interactions and reduce the tendency to withdraw. Practice mindfulness techniques, such as focused breathing or body scanning, to ground yourself in the moment and fully engage with your partner.

Imagine someone like Daniel, who struggles with avoidant attachment. Daniel finds it difficult to share his feelings and often avoids deep conversations. He decides to start journaling about his fears, uncovering past experiences contributing to his avoidance. Daniel aims to share one personal story with his partner each week. He also practices mindfulness to stay present during their conversations.

As Daniel continues his journey, he finds that journaling not only helps him understand his fears but also allows him to process emotions he previously suppressed. He begins to recognize patterns in his avoidance, often triggered by memories of childhood emotional neglect. With this awareness, Daniel starts to challenge his automatic responses to emotional intimacy.

The weekly sharing of personal stories becomes a cornerstone of Daniel's growth. Initially, he struggles to open up, often feeling vulnerable and exposed. However, his partner's consistent supportive responses gradually reinforce that emotional sharing is safe and valued. Daniel's mindfulness practice proves instrumental in managing the anxiety that arises during these moments of vulnerability. By focusing on his breath and bodily sensations, he learns to stay grounded in the present, rather than retreating into his habitual emotional distance.

As months pass, Daniel's efforts begin to yield significant results. He finds himself initiating deeper conversations more frequently, and the fear of emotional intimacy, while still present, no longer paralyzes him. His relationship takes on a new depth, characterized by mutual understanding and shared vulnerability. Daniel's journey illustrates how consistent, intentional effort can transform deeply ingrained attachment patterns, leading to more fulfilling and secure relationships.

Healing Disorganized Attachment Patterns

Disorganized attachment can feel like being caught in a whirlwind of emotions. If you have this attachment style, you might exhibit erratic and unpredictable behaviors, making it difficult for you and your partner to find stability. One moment, you could be craving closeness; the next, you might be pushing your partner away. This inconsistency often stems from a childhood where caregivers were both a source of comfort and fear, creating a confusing emotional landscape. Difficulty regulating emotions is another hallmark of disorganized attachment. You might experience intense emotional highs and lows, finding it challenging to maintain a balanced state. This rollercoaster of emotions can be exhausting, leaving you feeling out of control and overwhelmed.

Additionally, you may harbor a deep fear of both abandonment and closeness. The thought of being left alone terrifies you, but the idea of letting someone get too close can be equally frightening. This internal conflict makes it hard to trust others and build stable relationships.

The impact of disorganized attachment on relationships is profound. Your conflicted feelings towards your partners can create a chaotic dynamic. You might oscillate between intense closeness and extreme distance, leaving your partner confused and unsure of where they stand. These emotional highs and lows can make the relationship feel like a constant battle, draining you and your partner. Trust becomes a significant challenge. You might need help to believe that your partner has your best interests at heart, leading to frequent misunderstandings and conflicts. Stability feels like an elusive goal, as the erratic nature of your attachment style makes it hard to establish a steady, secure connection.

Healing from disorganized attachment requires a multi-faceted approach. Trauma-informed therapy can be incredibly beneficial. Therapies such as EMDR (Eye Movement Desensitization and Reprocessing) or Somatic Experiencing focus on resolving the root causes of your attachment issues. These therapies help you process and integrate traumatic experiences, reducing their impact on your current behavior. Developing consistent routines can also provide a sense of stability. Establish daily habits that promote emotional well-being, such as regular exercise, healthy eating, and sufficient sleep. These routines create a predictable structure, helping you feel more grounded. Building a support network is another critical step. Surround yourself with people who understand your struggles and can offer consistent emotional support. Family, trusted friends, or support groups can provide a safe space to express your feelings and gain perspective.

Consider incorporating specific exercises into your daily life to manage disorganized attachment behaviors. Grounding techniques can help you regulate your emotions. When you feel overwhelmed, take a moment to focus on your senses. Notice the texture of an object, the sounds around you, or the feeling of your feet on the ground. This practice can anchor you in the present moment, reducing the intensity of your emotions. Journaling is another effective tool for processing conflicting emotions. Write about your experiences, feelings, and thoughts without judgment. This practice can help you make sense of your feelings and identify patterns in your behavior. Mindfulness practices can also promote stability. Spend a few minutes each day focusing on your breath or mindfulness meditation. This practice can help you develop greater emotional resilience and better manage stress.

Imagine someone like Laura, who struggles with disorganized attachment. She often feels torn between wanting to be close to her partner and fearing that closeness. Laura decides to seek trauma-informed therapy, where she learns techniques to process her past experiences. She also sets a consistent daily routine, including morning exercise and evening journaling.

Laura's journey towards secure attachment is marked by challenges and breakthroughs. In therapy, she uncovers childhood experiences of inconsistent caregiving that contributed to her conflicted feelings about intimacy. Through EMDR and Somatic Experiencing techniques, Laura begins to process these early traumas, gradually reducing their impact on her current relationships.

Her daily routine becomes a cornerstone of her healing process. Morning exercises, particularly yoga and running, help Laura connect with her body and regulate her nervous system. Evening journaling provides a space to reflect on her emotions and interactions, allowing her to identify patterns in her behavior and responses.

As Laura progresses, she learns to recognize her attachment triggers. When she feels the urge to push her partner away, she practices grounding techniques learned in therapy. She begins to communicate her needs and fears more openly, surprising herself with her growing ability to be vulnerable.

Laura's partner notices the changes, commenting on her increased emotional availability and consistency. There are still difficult moments, but Laura finds she can navigate them with more clarity and less reactivity. She starts to trust not just her partner, but also her own emotions and instincts.

The transformation in Laura's relationships extends beyond her romantic partnership. She finds herself forming deeper friendships and improving family relationships as well. While she acknowledges that healing is an ongoing process, Laura feels a sense of pride and hope in her journey towards secure attachment.

Building Secure Attachment through Self-Compassion

Self-compassion plays a pivotal role in developing a secure attachment style. Treating yourself with kindness and under-standing creates a nurturing internal environment that fosters emotional resilience and self-acceptance. Reducing self-criticism is a crucial aspect of self-compassion. Instead of criticizing yourself for perceived flaws or mistakes, self-compassion encourages you to respond gently. This shift in perspective helps diminish the harsh inner critic that often fuels anxiety and insecurity in relationships. By being kinder to yourself, you build a foundation of self-worth that supports healthier interactions with others.

Enhancing emotional resilience is another significant benefit of self-compassion. When you face challenges or setbacks, self-compassion provides the emotional support needed to navigate these difficulties without becoming overwhelmed. It helps you bounce back more quickly and maintain a balanced emotional state. This resilience is crucial in relationships, where conflicts and misunderstandings are inevitable. You can handle situations more constructively by approaching them with a compassionate mindset. Promoting self-acceptance is also essential. Self-compassion allows you to embrace your imperfections and acknowledge that everyone makes mistakes. This acceptance fosters a sense of inner peace and reduces the fear of rejection, which can be particularly powerful for those with an anxious attachment style.

You can incorporate several practical exercises into your daily routine to cultivate self-compassion. Loving-kindness meditation is a powerful practice that involves sending positive wishes to yourself and others. Find a quiet place to sit comfortably, close your eyes, and take a few deep breaths. Repeat these phrases silently: 'May I be happy. May I be healthy. May I be safe. May I live with ease.' Gradually extend these wishes to include loved ones, acquaintances, and even people you find challenging. This practice helps foster a sense of compassion and connection with yourself and others. Self-compassionate journaling is another effective exercise. Set aside time each day to write about your experiences, focusing on areas where you can offer yourself kindness and understanding. Reflect on moments of difficulty and consider how you can respond to yourself with compassion. Practicing self-kindness in daily life is also crucial. This can be as simple as taking a break when you feel overwhelmed, speaking to yourself gently, or acknowledging your efforts and achievements.

The benefits of self-compassion for relationship dynamics are profound. Improved communication and empathy are among the most significant advantages. You become more attuned to your needs and emotions when you practice self-compassion. This self-awareness enables you to communicate more openly and honestly with your partner. Additionally, self-compassion enhances your ability to empathize with your partner's experiences, fostering a deeper connection and understanding. Excellent emotional stability is another critical benefit. Treating yourself with kindness creates a stable emotional foundation that reduces the intensity of emotional highs and lows. This stability helps you navigate conflicts and challenges more effectively, reducing conflict and misunderstandings in your relationship.

Consider the story of Ava, who struggled with low self-esteem and relationship anxiety. She often felt unworthy of love and harshly criticized herself for her shortcomings. Ava decided to practice loving-kindness meditation daily and began journaling her thoughts and feelings.

In the beginning, Ava found it challenging to sit with her thoughts during meditation, often battling against a barrage of self-criticism. However, she persevered, starting with just five minutes a day and gradually increasing the duration. As weeks passed, Ava began to notice subtle changes in her inner dialogue.

Her journaling practice became a powerful tool for self-discovery. Initially, her entries were filled with self-doubt and negativity. But as she continued writing, Ava started to identify patterns in her thinking. She challenged her negative self-talk, replacing harsh judgments with more compassionate perspectives.

Ava's growing self-awareness had a profound impact on her relationship. She realized how her fear of abandonment had been causing her to withdraw emotionally from her partner. With her newfound courage, Ava opened up about her insecurities. To her surprise, this vulnerability strengthened their bond.

As her self-esteem improved, Ava found herself setting healthy boundaries in her relationship and other areas of her life. She started pursuing long-forgotten hobbies and nurturing friendships that had been neglected. This renewed sense of self brought a new dynamic to her partnership, fostering mutual growth and respect.

Though she still experienced moments of self-doubt, Ava now had the tools to navigate these challenges. Her journey of self-discovery not only transformed her relationship but also opened up new possibilities in her personal and professional life. Ava's story exemplifies how self-compassion and consistent inner work can lead to profound changes in one's life and relationships.

Another example is David, who dealt with chronic anxiety and avoidance behaviors. By practicing self-compassionate journaling and incorporating mindfulness into his daily routine, David learned to accept his imperfections and reduce his self-criticism. This newfound self-acceptance allowed him to develop a more secure attachment style, leading to healthier and more fulfilling relationships.

Case Studies of Transitioning to Secure Attachment

Case studies show how people apply strategies to develop secure attachment styles in real life. They provide practical insights and inspire hope and motivation. When you examine the journeys of individuals who have successfully transitioned to secure attachment, you can see how to apply various techniques in real-life scenarios. These stories highlight the challenges faced, the strategies employed, and the personal growth achieved, making the process relatable and attainable.

Consider the story of Audrey, a young woman who struggled with anxious attachment. Her background was filled with inconsistency and emotional neglect, leaving her constantly seeking reassurance in her relationships. Audrey's initial challenges included a fear of abandonment and an overwhelming need for constant validation from her partner. She often felt that she was not enough, which led to frequent conflicts and emotional turmoil. To address these issues, Audrey began practicing mindfulness meditation to calm her anxiety and started journaling to track and challenge her negative thoughts. She also attended therapy sessions, where she learned to build her self-worth and enhance her communication skills. Over time, Audrey's anxiety diminished, and she developed a more secure attachment style. She became more confident in her values and could communicate her needs without fear. Her relationship flourished, leading to a deeper, more fulfilling connection with her partner.

Then there's Jack, who exhibited avoidant attachment behaviors. Raised in an environment where emotional expression was discouraged, Jack learned to rely solely on himself. His initial challenges included emotional distancing and a reluctance to commit, which made it difficult for him to form meaningful relationships. Jack's turning point came when he realized that his avoidance was preventing him from experiencing true intimacy. He began journaling about his fears of intimacy, gradually sharing personal details with his partner, and practicing empathy and active listening. Jack also set small, achievable goals for emotional openness, such as expressing a simple feeling or sharing a personal story.

At first, the idea of opening up felt foreign and uncomfortable. His journal entries were brief and guarded, reflecting his ingrained habit of emotional suppression. However, as he persisted, Jack began to uncover the roots of his avoidance. He recognized how his childhood experiences had shaped his belief that vulnerability was a weakness.

Gradually, Jack started to implement small changes in his daily interactions. He set a goal to share personal thoughts or feelings with his partner regularly. Initially, these revelations were surface-level, but over time, Jack found the courage to delve deeper. He was surprised to find that his partner's supportive responses helped alleviate his fear of rejection.

Practicing empathy and active listening proved to be transformative for Jack. As he learned to truly hear and validate his partner's emotions, he found it easier to connect with his own feelings. This newfound emotional awareness began to spill over into other areas of his life, improving his relationships with friends and family.

There were times for Jack when he felt the urge to retreat into his shell, especially during conflicts or moments of stress. However, he had developed tools to recognize and challenge these avoidant tendencies. Through consistent effort and self-reflection, Jack cultivated a more secure attachment style, finding a balance between his need for independence and his desire for emotional connections.

Another compelling case is that of Abby, who struggled with disorganized attachment. Her childhood was marked by unpredictability and emotional chaos, leading to erratic and unpredictable behaviors in her relationships. Abby's initial challenges included intense emotional highs and lows, conflicted feelings towards her partners, and difficulty regulating her emotions. To address these issues, Abby sought trauma-informed therapy, where she learned techniques to process her past experiences. She also developed consistent daily routines, such as regular exercise and mindfulness practices, to create a sense of stability. Building a support network of trusted friends provided her with consistent emotional support. These strategies helped Abby manage her emotions more effectively, leading to a more secure attachment style. She experienced more excellent stability in her relationships as she learned to trust her partners and communicate her needs more clearly.

These case studies reveal common themes and valuable lessons. Self-awareness and self-compassion are fundamental to the process of developing secure attachment. The first step is to recognize your attachment style and its impact on your relationships. Consistent effort and practice are crucial. The journey towards secure attachment is gradual and requires patience and persistence. Regularly practicing strategies such as mindfulness, journaling, and open communication can lead to significant improvements over time. Support networks and professional help play a vital role. Surrounding yourself with supportive individuals and seeking therapy can provide the guidance and encouragement needed to navigate the challenges of attachment issues.

From these case studies, several actionable insights and tips emerge. Setting realistic and achievable goals is essential. Break down your objectives into manageable steps, and celebrate small victories. Practicing patience and persistence is crucial. Developing a secure attachment style takes time and effort, and be kind to yourself throughout the process. Seeking support and guidance when needed is vital. Don't hesitate to contact trusted friends, family members, or therapists for help and encouragement. These resources can provide valuable perspective and support as you work towards building healthier, more secure relationships.

In summary, transitioning to a secure attachment style involves understanding your attachment patterns, applying practical strategies, and seeking support. By learning from real-life examples and incorporating these insights into your life, you can develop healthier, more fulfilling relationships. This journey is a testament to the power of self-awareness, self-compassion, and consistent effort. As you continue to build secure attachments, you'll find that your relationships become more stable, supportive, and enriching.

CHAPTER SIX

Effective Communication and Setting Boundaries

Imagine this: You're conversing with your partner, and you've just shared something deeply personal. You wait for a response, but instead of feeling heard, you sense a wall. They're distracted, maybe scrolling through their phone or their mind elsewhere. You feel dismissed, unseen, and alone. This scenario, though common, can erode the foundation of any relationship. Effective communication, particularly active listening, is a cornerstone of healthy relationships. It's about genuinely hearing and understanding your partner, creating a space where you can connect and feel valued.

The Art of Active Listening

Active listening is more than just hearing words; it's about engaging fully with the person speaking and making them feel understood. In relationships, this form of listening reduces misunderstandings, builds trust, and enhances empathy. When you actively listen, you make fewer assumptions and errors in understanding, which means fewer conflicts. Misunderstandings often arise when one feels unheard or misinterpreted, but active listening bridges these gaps. It creates a foundation of trust, as your partner feels valued and acknowledged. This, in turn, fosters a deeper connection and mutual respect. Enhancing empathy is another critical benefit. You step into your partner's shoes by genuinely listening and gaining insight into their feelings and perspectives. This empathy strengthens your bond, allowing you to support each other more effectively.

Key components make up the essence of active listening. Paying full attention is paramount. This means setting aside distractions, making eye contact, and focusing entirely on the speaker. It's about being present in the moment and showing your partner that they are your priority. Reflecting on what is heard is another crucial element. This involves paraphrasing or summarizing your partner's words to ensure you've understood correctly. For instance, you might say, "So what I'm hearing is that you felt hurt when I didn't call back." This reflection demonstrates that you're engaged and genuinely trying to understand their perspective. Avoiding interruptions is equally essential. Let your partner finish their thoughts without cutting in, even if you have something important to add. Interruptions can make the speaker feel rushed or undervalued, disrupting the flow of communication.

To practice active listening, consider incorporating specific techniques. Using verbal affirmations like "I understand" or

"Tell me more" encourages your partner to continue sharing. These phrases show that you're interested and engaged. Non-verbal cues such as nodding and maintaining eye contact also play a significant role. These gestures signal attentiveness and respect, reinforcing your verbal affirmations. Paraphrasing and summarizing what your partner has said helps clarify and confirm understanding. If your partner explains a tough day at work, you might respond, "It sounds like you had a stressful day. That must have been challenging." This not only shows you're listening but also that you empathize with their experience.

Exercises help you develop and enhance active listening skills. Role-playing listening scenarios with a friend or partner can be highly effective. Take turns sharing stories or concerns, focusing on applying active listening techniques. After each session, provide feedback on what worked well and what could be improved. Practicing active listening with a partner in everyday conversations also reinforces these skills. Make a conscious effort to fully engage during routine discussions about daily plans or deeper emotional topics. Self-reflection on listening habits can further aid in improvement. After a conversation, take a moment to assess your performance. Did you interrupt? Were you entirely present? What could you do better next time? This self-awareness helps you identify areas for growth and refine your skills.

Active listening transforms communication in relationships, fostering understanding, trust, and empathy. By fully engaging with your partner, reflecting on their words, and avoiding interruptions, you create a space where both of you feel heard and valued. These techniques and exercises can help you build stronger, more meaningful connections, paving the way for healthier and more fulfilling relationships.

Expressing Your Needs Without Fear

Expressing your needs in a relationship is crucial for several reasons. When you communicate your needs clearly, you prevent resentment from building up. Imagine bottling up your feelings because you fear your partner's reaction. Over time, these unexpressed needs can turn into frustration, leading to resentment. Resentment is like a slow poison, eroding the foundation of your relationship. It creates a barrier between you and your partner, making it difficult to connect and understand each other. You release this built-up tension by expressing your needs, creating a healthier dynamic.

Building mutual respect is another significant benefit of expressing your needs. When you voice your needs, you show that you value yourself and your well-being. This self-respect encourages your partner to respect you as well. Setting boundaries establishes how you expect others to treat you, promoting a balanced and respectful relationship. Mutual respect is the critical for any healthy relationship. It ensures that both partners feel valued and understood, fostering a sense of equality and partnership.

Clear communication directly enhances relationship satisfaction. When you share your needs, your partner knows how to better support you. This understanding leads to greater emotional and physical satisfaction in the relationship. You create a space where you can thrive, feeling loved and appreciated. When partners meet each other's needs, they create a more fulfilling and resilient relationship that can weather challenges and grow stronger over time.

To express your needs assertively, use specific techniques. One effective method is using "I" statements. Phrases like "I feel" or "I need" focus on your needs and feelings rather than blaming your partner. Instead of saying, "You never listen to me," try saying, "I feel unheard when we don't discuss things openly." This approach reduces defensiveness and opens up a more constructive dialogue. Being specific and clear is also essential. Vague statements can lead to misunderstandings. If you need more quality time, say, "I would love to spend an hour together after dinner each day," rather than a general, "We need to spend more time together." Clarity ensures that your partner knows exactly what you need, making it easier for them to respond appropriately.

Avoiding blame or criticism is crucial when expressing needs. Blaming your partner can put them on the defensive, shutting down effective communication. Instead, focus on how the situation affects you and what you need to feel better. For example, instead of saying, "You never help with the chores," try, "I feel overwhelmed when I have to handle all the chores alone. Can we find a way to share them more evenly?" This approach fosters collaboration and problem-solving rather than conflict.

Let's look at specific scenarios to illustrate how to express different needs. For emotional needs, imagine you're going through a tough time at work. You might tell your partner, "I've been feeling stressed at work lately. It would mean a lot to me if you could spend extra time talking with me in the evenings." This clear and heartfelt request helps your partner understand your emotional support needs. You need personal space to recharge for physical needs after a long day. You could say, "I need some quiet time when I get home to unwind. Can we plan to have some alone time before we start our evening together?" This request communicates your need for personal space without making your partner feel rejected. For practical needs, let's say you need help with household chores. You might say, "I feel overwhelmed with all the housework. Can we create a schedule to share the chores more evenly?" This approach makes your need for practical support clear and actionable.

Overcoming the fear of expressing your needs can be challenging, but effective strategies to build confidence exist. Practicing self-affirmation is one such strategy. Remind yourself regularly that your needs are valid and essential. Positive affirmations like "I deserve to have my needs met" can boost your confidence over time. Rehearsing conversations in a safe environment can also help. Practice expressing your needs with a trusted friend or even in front of a mirror. This rehearsal can make the actual conversation feel more manageable. Another practical approach is to start with small, low-stakes requests. Begin by expressing needs in less critical situations to build your confidence. As you become more comfortable, gradually move on to more significant requests.

Expressing your needs without fear is vital for maintaining a healthy and fulfilling relationship. By preventing resentment, building mutual respect, and enhancing relationship satisfaction, you create a strong foundation for your partnership. Using techniques like "I" statements, being specific and clear, and avoiding blame or criticism can make the process smoother. Practicing self-affirmation, rehearsing conversations, and starting with small requests can help you overcome the fear of voicing your needs.

Setting Healthy Boundaries in Relationships

Healthy boundaries are like invisible lines that protect your personal space, emotions, and well-being. They help maintain balanced relationships by ensuring that partners respect each other's limits. When you set boundaries, you protect your well-being by meeting your needs without sacrificing yourself. These boundaries help you maintain a sense of self, which is crucial for mental and emotional health. They also enhance mutual respect in the relationship. By clearly defining what is acceptable and what is not, both partners learn to respect each other's limits, fostering a sense of equality and partnership. Another significant benefit is preventing burnout and resentment. Without boundaries, you might find yourself constantly giving without receiving, leading to emotional exhaustion and resentment. Setting clear boundaries helps ensure that the relationship remains balanced and healthy.

There are different types of boundaries that you can set in relationships. Physical boundaries pertain to personal space and physical touch. For example, you might need time alone to recharge after a long day or prefer a certain amount of personal space even when you're with your partner. Emotional boundaries involve the sharing of feelings and emotions. Deciding how much emotional energy you can invest in your partner without feeling overwhelmed is essential. Time boundaries are about managing your time effectively. Set aside specific times for yourself, work, or hobbies, ensuring a balanced life outside the relationship. Material boundaries concern the sharing of possessions. For instance, you might feel uncomfortable lending your car or personal items and must communicate this to your partner.

Identifying and setting healthy boundaries involves a few crucial steps. First, identify your limits and needs. Reflect on what makes you feel uncomfortable or stressed in your relationship. It could be anything from needing more alone time to wanting your partner to respect your belongings. Once you've identified these limits, the next step is communicating them. Use "I" statements to express your boundaries without blaming or criticizing your partner. For example, you might say, "I need some quiet time to recharge after work," instead of "You're always bothering me when I get home." Clear communication helps your partner understand your needs without feeling attacked. Enforcing boundaries consistently is equally important. Your partner may not take it seriously if you set a boundary but don't stick to it. Make sure to uphold your boundaries even if it feels challenging. Consistency reinforces the importance of your limits and helps maintain respect.

Let's look at specific scenarios to illustrate setting and maintaining boundaries effectively. Imagine you're feeling overwhelmed with additional responsibilities at work and home. You should say no to taking on more tasks from your partner. You could express this by saying, "I'm feeling overwhelmed right now and can't take on additional tasks. Can we find a way to share the responsibilities more evenly?" This clear communication helps your partner understand your limits and work towards a solution together. Requesting alone time is another common boundary that many people need. If you need personal space to unwind, you might say, "I need time alone each evening to relax and recharge. Can we set aside an hour each day for personal time?" This request helps you maintain your well-being without making your partner feel rejected. Setting limits on emotional sharing is also crucial, especially if you're a highly sensitive person (HSP). You should protect your emotional energy by limiting the amount of emotional support you provide. You could say, "I want to support you, but I'm feeling emotionally drained right now. Can we discuss this later when I'm in a better place to help?"

Healthy boundaries protect personal well-being, enhance mutual respect, and prevent burnout and resentment. You create a balanced and respectful relationship by identifying personal limits, communicating them clearly, and enforcing them consistently. Setting and maintaining these boundaries ensures that both partners feel valued and understood, fostering a healthier and more fulfilling connection.

Conflict Resolution Techniques

Effective conflict resolution is paramount for maintaining healthy relationships. When conflicts arise, addressing them constructively can prevent escalation, promote understanding, and strengthen the bond between partners. Imagine a scenario where a minor disagreement about household chores spirals into a full-blown argument. If left unresolved, such conflicts can lead to resentment and emotional distance. By resolving conflicts constructively, you prevent minor issues from escalating into major problems. This approach fosters understanding, as both partners feel heard and validated. When conflicts are addressed and resolved, the relationship becomes stronger, built on a foundation of trust and mutual respect.

There are several techniques for resolving conflicts effectively. Active listening is a fundamental method. It involves fully engaging with your partner, understanding their perspective, and reflecting on what you've heard. This technique ensures that both partners feel heard and understood. Compromise and negotiation are also essential. Finding a middle ground where both partners can be satisfied is critical to any relationship. This might involve making concessions or finding creative solutions that meet both partners' needs. Problem-solving approaches are another valuable technique. This method consists of identifying the root cause of the conflict, brainstorming possible solutions, and agreeing on a plan of action. You can address the issue constructively by focusing on solutions rather than blame.

To resolve conflicts effectively, follow a step-by-step guide. First, identify the issue. Take the time to understand what the conflict is really about. This might involve peeling back the layers of the argument to uncover the underlying problem. For example, disagreements about household chores are about feeling unappreciated or overwhelmed. Next, express your feelings and needs assertively. Use "I" statements to communicate your feelings and needs. For instance, "I feel overwhelmed when I have to decide on, prepare, and clean up dinner every night. I need us to share these responsibilities." This approach reduces defensiveness and opens up a constructive dialogue. Then, find common ground and mutual solutions. Work together to brainstorm possible solutions that meet both partners' needs. This might involve making compromises or finding creative ways to address the issue. For example, you might agree to create a chore schedule that ensures both partners contribute equally.

Let's explore some specific scenarios to illustrate effective conflict resolution techniques. Imagine a couple struggling with disagreements over household chores. One partner feels overwhelmed with the responsibilities, while the other feels they are doing their fair share. To resolve this conflict, they first identify the issue clearly: the imbalance in chore distribution. They express their feelings and needs assertively. One partner says, "I feel exhausted and unappreciated when I handle most of the chores. I need us to share the workload more evenly." The other partner might respond, "I didn't realize you felt that way. I'm willing to help more, but I need clear instructions on what needs to be done." Together, they find common ground by creating a chore schedule that outlines each partner's responsibilities, ensuring a fair distribution of tasks.

In another scenario, a couple faces conflicts about financial decisions. One partner is a spender, while the other is a saver. They identify the issue clearly to resolve this conflict: differing financial priorities. They express their feelings and needs assertively. The saver says, "I feel anxious when we spend money on non-essentials. I need us to have a budget that prioritizes savings." The spender might respond, "I understand your concerns, but I also need us to have some flexibility for enjoyment." They create a budget that allocates a certain amount for savings and a smaller amount for discretionary spending, finding common ground and meeting both partners' needs.

Navigating differences in parenting styles is another common source of conflict. One partner might favor a more lenient approach, while the other prefers strict discipline. They identify the issue clearly to resolve this conflict: differing parenting philosophies. They express their feelings and needs assertively. One partner says, "I feel concerned when we don't have consistent rules for our children. I need us to agree on a discipline strategy." The other partner might respond, "I understand your concerns, but I also want our children to feel loved and supported." They find common ground by discussing and agreeing on a balanced approach that combines structure with support, ensuring a consistent and nurturing environment for their children.

Scripts for Difficult Conversations

Having difficult conversations is crucial in any relationship. These challenging discussions address unresolved issues, prevent misunderstandings, and strengthen communication. Imagine feeling hurt because your partner consistently overlooks your needs. Without discussing it openly, resentment builds, creating a barrier that prevents genuine connection. Addressing these topics head-on allows both partners to understand each other's perspectives, fostering a deeper bond. It also prevents misunderstandings. When issues remain unspoken, assumptions fill the gaps, often leading to conflicts based on misconceptions. Clear communication cuts through this fog, ensuring both parties are on the same page. Strengthening communication through difficult conversations builds a robust foundation for the relationship. It teaches both partners how to navigate challenges together, enhancing mutual respect and understanding.

Preparing for difficult conversations requires thoughtful planning. Start by choosing the right time and place. Find a quiet, private setting where you won't be interrupted. Timing is also crucial. Avoid moments when either of you is stressed or distracted. Plan key points you want to discuss. Outline your thoughts so you can articulate them clearly. This preparation helps you stay focused and ensures you cover all necessary topics. Staying calm and focused during the conversation is essential. Take deep breaths if you feel anxious. Keep your tone even and avoid raising your voice, which can escalate tensions.

To assist you, here are some scripts for common difficult conversations. When addressing unmet needs, you might say, "I feel hurt when my needs are not met. It makes me feel unappreciated and undervalued." This statement clearly expresses your feelings without placing blame. For discussing boundaries, you could use, "I need more personal space to recharge. It helps me feel more balanced and present in our relationship." This communicates your need for space without making your partner feel rejected. Handling conflicts might involve saying, "I would like to discuss our disagreement calmly. I think it's important for us to understand each other's perspectives and find a solution together." This approach emphasizes the importance of mutual understanding and collaboration.

Successfully navigating difficult conversations involves several strategies. Use active listening to show you value your partner's perspective. Reflect on what they're saying to ensure you understand correctly. Stay open to feedback. Be willing to hear your partner's side and consider their feelings and needs. This openness fosters mutual respect and understanding. Acknowledge and validate the other person's feelings. Saying something like, "I understand that you feel upset about this," can go a long way in making your partner feel heard and respected.

Incorporating these elements into your conversations creates a space where both partners feel safe to express themselves. It transforms potentially contentious discussions into opportunities for growth and deeper connection. You build a more resilient and fulfilling relationship by addressing unresolved issues, preventing misunderstandings, and strengthening communication.

Maintaining Boundaries Over Time

Consistently maintaining boundaries is crucial for ensuring personal well-being, promoting mutual respect, and preventing boundary erosion. When you enforce boundaries regularly, you safeguard your mental and emotional health. Boundaries protect you and ensure you meet your needs without others overshadowing them. They promote mutual respect within relationships, teaching both partners to value and honor each other's limits. Boundaries can become blurred without consistent enforcement, leading to misunderstandings and conflicts. Over time, this boundary erosion can result in feelings of resentment or being taken for granted, making it essential to keep boundaries clear and intact.

Regular boundary check-ins are vital in maintaining them over time. These check-ins allow you to assess whether others respect your boundaries and whether you need to make any adjustments. Set aside time to discuss boundaries with your partner, ensuring you are on the same page. Communicating changes in boundaries is also essential. As relationships evolve, so do your needs and limits. Communicate this change to your partner if a boundary needs to be adjusted. Reinforcing boundaries is critical to maintaining their effectiveness. Stand firm on your limits and prevent others from crossing them. If a boundary is violated, address it immediately and reiterate its importance.

Common challenges in maintaining boundaries can arise, making it difficult to uphold them consistently. Pushback from others is a frequent obstacle. When you set a boundary, some people might resist or challenge it, mainly if they are used to having more access to your time and energy. Feeling guilty or selfish is another common challenge. You might struggle with the belief that setting boundaries is selfish or that you're letting others down. This guilt can make it difficult to enforce your limits consistently. Boundary violations, whether intentional or accidental, can also pose a challenge. When someone crosses your boundary, addressing the violation without causing conflict can be challenging.

Overcoming these challenges requires a combination of strategies. Practicing self-compassion is essential. Remember that your needs are valid and that setting boundaries is a form of self-care. Treat yourself with the same kindness and understanding that you would offer a friend in a similar situation. Seeking support from trusted friends or therapists can also help. Discussing your boundaries and challenges with supportive individuals can give you encouragement and perspective. They can offer advice and reinforce the importance of maintaining your limits. Staying firm and consistent is crucial. Even when faced with pushback or guilt, remain steadfast in upholding your boundaries. When you consistently enforce your boundaries, you reinforce their importance and ensure others respect them over time.

Imagine you've set a boundary to have an hour of alone time each evening to recharge. Initially, your partner respects this, but over time, they begin to interrupt this time with requests or conversations. To maintain this boundary, schedule regular check-ins to discuss how it's working and whether any adjustments are needed. If you notice your partner frequently interrupting, communicate this change. You might say, "I've noticed we aren't respecting our alone time boundary as much. It's important for my well-being, so I need us to stick to it." If you feel guilty about enforcing this boundary, practice self-compassion. Remember that caring for your needs is not selfish but necessary for your well-being. Seek support from a friend who understands the importance of personal time. If a boundary violation occurs, address it assertively but calmly. You might say, "I need my alone time to recharge. Can we discuss this after my hour is up?"

When you maintain boundaries over time, you ensure that you meet your needs, promote mutual respect, and prevent the erosion of those boundaries. Regular check-ins, clear communication of changes, and assertive reinforcement are essential strategies. Overcoming challenges like pushback, guilt, and boundary violations requires self-compassion, support from trusted individuals, and consistency. Maintaining your boundaries effectively creates a healthier, more balanced relationship where both partners feel valued and respected.

In our next chapter, we will explore how to build self-esteem and confidence, essential components for sustaining emotional growth and healthy relationships. By understanding and maintaining boundaries, expressing needs, and resolving conflicts effectively, you lay the groundwork for a strong, fulfilling partnership.

CHAPTER SEVEN

Building Self-Esteem and Confidence

Have you ever stood in front of a mirror, looking at your reflection but feeling like a stranger is staring back at you? It's a moment that can be both unsettling and revealing. I remember standing there, scrutinizing every detail, and feeling an overwhelming sense of inadequacy. It wasn't just about physical appearance; it was about a deep-seated belief that I wasn't enough. This chapter helps you transform moments of self-doubt into affirmations of self-worth.

Daily Affirmations for Self-Worth

Affirmations are powerful assertions that can reprogram your mind to think more positively about yourself. They are simple yet profound tools that can reshape your mental landscape. When you repeat affirmations, you challenge and replace negative thought patterns. Imagine the impact of telling yourself, "I am worthy of love and respect," every day. This repetition helps to reinforce positive self-beliefs, gradually shifting your mindset from doubt to confidence.

Daily affirmations reprogram negative thought patterns that have become ingrained over time. If you constantly tell yourself that you are not good enough, your mind starts to believe it. Affirmations counteract these negative messages by providing a positive alternative. For example, if you often think, "I'm not capable," repeating the affirmation, "I believe in my abilities and strengths," can help you start to see yourself differently. This shift in thinking enhances your confidence, making you more resilient in the face of challenges.

To make affirmations a part of your daily routine, be consistent. Incorporate them into your morning and evening routines. Start your day by looking in the mirror and repeating your affirmations. This sets a positive tone for the day ahead. Before bed, take a moment to reflect on your day and repeat your affirmations. This practice can help to calm your mind and reinforce positive thoughts before sleep. Setting reminders on your phone can also be helpful. A notification that pops up with an affirmation can serve as a prompt to take a moment and focus on your self-worth. Using an affirmation journal is another effective method. Write down your affirmations each day and any thoughts or feelings that arise. This practice reinforces the affirmations and provides a record of your progress.

Personalizing your affirmations can make them even more powerful. Reflect on your values and desires. What qualities do you admire in yourself? What goals are you striving to achieve? Incorporate these specific elements into your affirmations. For example, if you value kindness, you might create an affirmation like, "I am kind and compassionate." If you've recently achieved something significant, include that in your affirmation. For instance, "I am proud of my accomplishments and believe in my potential." Crafting affirmations in your own words ensures they resonate deeply with you.

Here are a few affirmations to get you started:

"I am worthy of love and respect."

"I believe in my abilities and strengths."

"I am confident in who I am."

Reflect on what these statements mean to you personally. As you repeat them daily, notice the subtle shifts in your thoughts and feelings. Over time, these affirmations can help you build a stronger sense of self-worth and confidence.

Incorporating daily affirmations into your routine can transform the way you see yourself. You can reprogram your mind to embrace self-worth and confidence by consistently repeating positive statements. Personalizing your affirmations ensures they resonate deeply with your unique experiences and goals. Remember, you are worthy of love and respect and have the power to believe in your abilities and strengths.

Overcoming Insecurity and Jealousy

Insecurity and jealousy often stem from deep-rooted issues built up over time. Low self-esteem is one of the primary culprits. When you don't believe in your worth, it's easy to question why someone would be interested in you. This doubt seeps into your relationship, making you constantly seek validation from your partner. Past relationship traumas add another layer to this complex emotion. If you've been cheated on, lied to, or betrayed, those scars remain. They whisper doubts into your ear, making you wary and suspicious even when there's no reason to be. Lastly, comparing yourself to others can fuel insecurity and jealousy. In a world where social media showcases everyone's highlight reels, it's easy to feel like you don't measure up. You might think, "Why would my partner choose me over someone more attractive, successful, or interesting?"

Addressing these insecurities involves several actionable steps. Building self-awareness is the first step. Take time to reflect on your thoughts and feelings. When do you feel most insecure? What triggers these feelings? Write down your observations to identify patterns. Practicing self-affirmation is another powerful tool. Replace negative thoughts with positive ones. For instance, if you think, "I'm not good enough," counter it with, "I bring unique qualities to this relationship." Setting realistic expectations is also crucial. Understand that no one is perfect—not you or your partner. Accepting this can relieve some of the pressure you put on yourself and your relationship.

Jealousy, while natural, can be managed with the proper techniques. Open communication with your partner is vital. Share your feelings without accusing them. Use "I" statements like, "I feel insecure when you talk to your ex," instead of "You make me jealous when you talk to your ex." This approach fosters understanding and reduces defensiveness. Focusing on self-improvement can also help. Invest time in hobbies and activities that make you feel good about yourself. The more fulfilled you are individually, the less you will rely on your partner for validation. Avoiding comparisons is equally important. Remind yourself that everyone has their path and struggles. What you see on social media or others' lives is only part of the picture.

Real-life examples can offer valuable insights into overcoming these emotions. Anna's journey from jealousy to trust exemplifies the transformative power of self-awareness and therapeutic intervention. At 29, Anna found herself trapped in a cycle of suspicion and fear, her past experiences casting a shadow over her current relationship. Her behavior, characterized by constant phone-checking and interrogation, threatened to undermine the connection with her and her partner.

The turning point came when Anna recognized the destructive nature of her actions. Seeking professional help, she embarked on a path of healing and growth. Through therapy, Anna delved into the root causes of her jealousy, uncovering the lingering effects of past betrayal.

Key to Anna's progress was learning to distinguish between her traumatic memories and her present reality. She developed strategies to ground herself in the moment, challenging intrusive thoughts with rational evidence. Simultaneously, Anna cultivated open communication with her partner, bravely sharing her insecurities without accusation.

Anna saw success in a few months. Her compulsive checking behaviors decreased, replaced by a growing sense of security. She found herself able to trust her partner's words and actions, no longer viewing them through a lens of suspicion.

The impact of Anna's transformation extended beyond her romantic relationship. Her newfound trust and openness fostered deeper connections in all areas of her life. Anna's story stands as a testament to the possibility of overcoming deep-seated emotional challenges through self-reflection, professional guidance, and committed personal growth.

Next, take Mark, a 34, Marketing Coordinator who had career-related insecurity affecting his relationship dynamics. Mark felt significant insecurity from his partner's professional success. As a marketing coordinator, he perceived his career trajectory as less impressive compared to his partner's rapid advancement in corporate finance. This disparity led to chronic feelings of inadequacy and self-doubt, manifesting in frequent comparisons and subtle resentment within the relationship. Mark began to tackle his issues head on and started with cognitive restructuring exercises to challenge his self-deprecating thoughts. He implemented goal-setting techniques focused on personal growth rather than comparative success and introduced daily gratitude practices to acknowledge personal achievements. He realized he had to have open dialogue with his partner, and after a candid discussion, he realized that his career path was different but no less valuable. He developed a personalized career development plan, setting achievable short-term goals aligned with his interests and skills. This, along with the implementation of a daily gratitude journal significantly boosted Mark's self-esteem. He reported feeling more confident in professional settings and less threatened by his partner's accomplishments.

Mark now has decreased anxiety about career discussions and increased ability to celebrate his partner's successes genuinely. His relationship had a marked improvement as well, they enjoy enhanced communication and mutual support in their respective professional endeavors.

Many people face insecurity and jealousy but it doesn't have to control their lives or relationships. By understanding their root causes and implementing strategies to manage them, you can build a healthier, more confident self. Open communication, self-improvement, and avoiding comparisons are critical steps in this journey. Remember, you are not alone in feeling this way; you can overcome these challenges with time and effort.

Embracing Your Authentic Self

Embracing your authentic self means living in alignment with your values, beliefs, and desires. It involves expressing yourself genuinely, without pretense or facade, and celebrating your unique qualities. Authenticity is the foundation of self-esteem and confidence because it allows you to live a life that feels true to who you are. When you embrace your authentic self, you stop trying to fit into molds created by societal expectations or the opinions of others. Instead, you live according to your standards, which fosters a deep sense of self-worth and fulfillment.

However, several barriers can make it challenging to embrace authenticity. One significant obstacle is the fear of judgment and rejection. Many worry that showing their true selves will lead to criticism or ostracism. This fear can make you hide parts of yourself that you think others won't accept. Societal pressures and expectations also play a role. From a young age, society often teaches us to conform to certain norms and behaviors to be accepted. These societal standards can stifle individuality and make you feel that you need to be someone you are not to be loved or valued. Internalized negative beliefs, often stemming from past experiences or critical voices from childhood, can also hinder authenticity. If others repeatedly tell you you are not good enough or your true self is flawed, you might internalize these messages and suppress your authentic self.

Living authentically requires practical strategies and conscious effort. Start by reflecting on your values and passions. Take time to identify what truly matters and brings you joy. This self-reflection can help you understand your core beliefs and guide your actions. Practicing self-expression in small steps can also be helpful. Begin by sharing your feelings with family or trusted friends. Gradually expand this practice to other areas of your life, such as your workplace or social circles. Surrounding yourself with supportive people who encourage and accept you as you are can create a safe environment for authenticity. These individuals can provide validation and support, making it easier to be yourself without fear of judgment.

Real-life examples can illustrate the transformative power of embracing authenticity. Consider the story of Zoe, who spent years trying to fit into the corporate world, suppressing her creative passions. She always felt out of place and unfulfilled. One day, Zoe decided to pursue her love for painting, even though she feared judgment from her peers. She started sharing her artwork on social media, receiving positive feedback, and connecting with like-minded individuals. Embracing her authentic self boosted her self-esteem and led her to a successful artist career. Zoe's story highlights how living authentically can lead to personal and professional fulfillment.

Embracing your authentic self is a journey that involves overcoming fears and societal pressures. By reflecting on your values, practicing self-expression, and surrounding yourself with supportive individuals, you can live in alignment with your true self. Zoe's stoy illustrates authenticity's profound benefits, from personal fulfillment to even societal impact. Remember, your authentic self is worthy of love and respect, and living genuinely is the key to building self-esteem and confidence.

Recognizing and Celebrating Your Strengths

Recognizing and celebrating your strengths is fundamental to building self-esteem and confidence. Acknowledging your abilities and achievements can significantly boost self-awareness, helping you understand what makes you unique and valuable. When you recognize your strengths, you enhance your self-worth, reminding yourself that you possess qualities worthy of admiration. This acknowledgment encourages personal growth by motivating you to leverage your strengths in various aspects of your life. It creates a positive feedback loop, where the more you recognize your strengths, the more confident you become and the more you are inclined to develop and utilize them.

To identify your strengths, start by reflecting on your past achievements. Take a moment to think about when you felt proud of yourself. What were you doing? What qualities and skills did you use to achieve those successes? Write these down and consider how they apply to other areas of your life. Seeking feedback from others can also be enlightening. Ask trusted friends, family members, or colleagues to share what they see as your strengths. Sometimes, others can see qualities in us that we might overlook. Strength assessment quizzes can also provide a structured way to identify your strengths. These quizzes often highlight areas you might have yet to consider and can offer a new perspective on your abilities.

Celebrating your strengths is just as important as recognizing them. One way to do this is by setting goals aligned with your strengths. If you have a knack for organizing, set a goal to lead a project at work that requires those skills. Sharing your strengths with others can also be empowering. Whether mentoring someone, participating in a community project, or simply offering your expertise to a friend, sharing your strengths can boost your confidence and reinforce your abilities. Incorporating your strengths into daily activities is another effective way to celebrate them. If you're good at problem-solving, look for opportunities in your daily life to tackle challenges head-on. You reaffirm their value and build your confidence by actively using your strengths.

Consider the story of Joseph, who always felt uncertain about his abilities. After reflecting on his past achievements, he realized that his strength lay in connecting with people and building solid relationships. He decided to leverage this strength by volunteering at a local community center, where he could mentor young adults. This experience boosted his confidence and reinforced his sense of self-worth. By focusing on his strengths, Joseph found new ways to contribute to his community and enhance his personal growth.

Another example is Elizabeth, who struggled with low self-esteem for years. Through feedback from her colleagues and friends, she discovered that her strength was her creativity. Elizabeth decided to set a goal to create a personal blog where she could showcase her creative writing and art. Sharing her work with a broader audience celebrated her creativity and helped her connect with others who appreciated her talents. This validation from her readers boosted her self-esteem and motivated her to continue pursuing her creative passions.

Recognizing and celebrating your strengths can transform how you see yourself and your abilities. You can identify what makes you unique by reflecting on past achievements, seeking feedback, and taking strength assessment quizzes. Setting goals, sharing your strengths with others, and incorporating them into daily activities can help you celebrate and maximize your abilities. Personal stories like those of Joseph and Elizabeth illustrate the positive impact of focusing on strengths and how it can lead to greater self-esteem and confidence.

Self-Compassion Techniques for Building Confidence

Practicing self-compassion can be a transformative step in building your confidence. When you show kindness and understanding, you reduce the harsh self-criticism that often undermines your self-esteem. Imagine the power of replacing the critical voice in your head with one that encourages and supports you. This shift can promote emotional resilience, allowing you to bounce back from setbacks quickly. Self-compassion encourages self-acceptance, helping you embrace your imperfections as part of your unique self. Treating yourself with the same gentleness you would offer a friend lays the foundation for lasting confidence and emotional stability.

One powerful self-compassion technique is loving-kindness meditation. This practice involves sending positive and loving thoughts to yourself and others. Find a quiet space where you can sit comfortably. Close your eyes and take a few deep breaths. Direct your attention inward, mentally reciting positive statements such as "I am worthy of happiness, health, safety, and peace." Gradually expand your focus, offering similar affirmations for others - first to those close to you, then to casual contacts, and eventually to individuals who test your patience. This practice can help you cultivate a sense of compassion and connection, not only towards others but also towards yourself.

Self-compassionate journaling is another effective technique. Set aside time each day to write about your experiences, focusing on areas where you can offer yourself kindness and understanding. Reflect on moments of difficulty and consider how you can respond to yourself with compassion. For example, if you made a mistake, write about what you learned from the experience and how you can grow from it instead of berating yourself. This practice can help you shift your perspective from self-criticism to self-compassion, fostering a more supportive inner dialogue.

Practicing self-kindness in daily life is also crucial. This can be as simple as taking a break when you feel overwhelmed, speaking to yourself gently, or acknowledging your efforts and achievements. For instance, if you feel stressed at work, take a moment to step outside and breathe deeply. Remind yourself that taking breaks is okay and that taking care of your well-being is essential. By incorporating these small acts of self-kindness into your routine, you reinforce the habit of treating yourself with compassion and respect.

The benefits of self-compassion for personal growth are far-reaching. Better emotional stability is one of the most significant advantages. When you practice self-compassion, you are better equipped to handle life's ups and downs without being overwhelmed by negative emotions. This stability can improve relationships as you become more patient and understanding with others. Enhanced personal well-being is another critical benefit. By reducing self-criticism and promoting self-acceptance, self-compassion can help you feel more content and at peace with yourself.

Consider the story of Claire, who struggled with low self-esteem and constant self-criticism. She decided to try loving-kindness meditation and self-compassionate journaling. At first, it felt awkward, but over time, Claire noticed a shift in her mindset. She began to see herself more positively and felt more resilient in facing challenges. Her relationships improved as she became more patient and understanding with her friends and family. Claire's story demonstrates the transformative power of self-compassion in building confidence and enhancing overall well-being.

Another example is William, who dealt with intense self-criticism due to past failures. He started practicing self-kindness by acknowledging his efforts and celebrating small achievements. William also incorporated self-compassionate journaling into his routine, reflecting on his experiences with a gentle and supportive attitude. Over time, William's confidence grew, and he felt more capable of pursuing his goals. His story highlights how self-compassion can lead to increased confidence and personal growth, even in the face of past setbacks.

Visualizing Your Best Self

Visualization is a powerful technique that can profoundly impact your self-belief and motivation. Creating a vivid mental image of your best self can enhance your confidence and clarify your goals and aspirations. Visualization encourages positive behavior by allowing you to rehearse the actions and outcomes you desire mentally. It's like a dress rehearsal for your mind, preparing you to step into the role of your most confident and capable self.

To start practicing effective visualization, set a clear intention. Decide what you want to achieve with your visualization.

It could be gaining confidence for an upcoming presentation, improving your performance in a sport, or simply feeling more self-assured in your daily interactions. Once you have a clear goal, find a quiet place where you won't be disturbed. Close your eyes and take a few deep breaths to relax your mind and body.

Next, create a vivid mental image of your best self. Picture yourself achieving your goal with confidence and ease. Imagine every detail as clearly as possible. If you're visualizing a successful presentation, see yourself standing tall, speaking clearly, and engaging your audience. Notice the expressions on their faces, the sound of your voice, and the feeling of confidence in your body. Incorporate sensory details to make the image more realistic. Feel the warmth of the spotlight, hear the applause, and sense the satisfaction of a job well done. The more detailed and vivid your visualization, the more powerful it will be.

Consistency is crucial in visualization practices. To see significant improvements, make visualization a part of your daily routine. Set specific times for practice, such as first thing in the morning or before bed. Combining visualization with other mindfulness practices, like meditation or deep breathing, can enhance effectiveness. For example, start your day with a few minutes of meditation to calm your mind, followed by a visualization session where you picture yourself navigating the day with confidence and ease.

Imagine a young athlete named Grace who struggled with self-doubt before her races. She decided to incorporate visualization into her training routine. Every night before bed, she spent a few minutes visualizing herself running the perfect race. She pictured the track, the starting gun, and the feeling of her feet hitting the ground with power and precision. She imagined crossing the finish line and hearing the roar of the crowd. Over time, Grace noticed a significant boost in her confidence. Her performance improved; she felt more prepared and focused during her races. Visualization helped Grace transform her self-doubt into self-belief, illustrating the profound impact of this practice.

Another example is the story of a business professional, Robert, who used visualization to overcome his fear of public speaking. Robert's job required frequent presentations, but his anxiety often got the better of him. He began to visualize himself speaking confidently in front of an audience. He imagined the room, the audience's encouraging faces, and the sound of his voice resonating with clarity and authority. Robert practiced this visualization daily, and gradually, his fear diminished. His presentations became more impactful, and his confidence soared. Robert's experience demonstrates how visualization can turn anxiety into competence, leading to personal and professional growth.

Visualizing your best self can be a transformative tool for boosting confidence and achieving your goals. By setting clear intentions, creating vivid mental images, and incorporating sensory details, you can harness the power of your mind to shape your reality. Consistency in practice is critical, and combining visualization with other mindfulness techniques can enhance its benefits. The stories of Grace and Robert highlight the effectiveness of visualization in overcoming challenges and building self-belief. As you embrace this practice, you'll find yourself stepping more confidently into the person you aspire to be.

CHAPTER EIGHT

Sustaining Emotional Growth and Healthy Relationships

You know those moments when you feel utterly exhausted, not from physical activity but from the emotional roller-coaster of life? One evening, I remember being overwhelmed by work demands, relationships, and personal expectations. I felt like I was running on empty, my emotional reserves wholly depleted. It was then I realized the importance of self-care—not just as a buzzword but as a vital practice for emotional well-being. Self-care is not an indulgence; it's a necessity. It's about taking deliberate actions to ensure you are mentally, emotionally, and physically healthy.

Developing a Self-Care Routine

Self-care is crucial for maintaining emotional stability and overall mental health. Engaging in regular self-care practices helps reduce stress and anxiety, which are common culprits in emotional turmoil. When you take time for yourself, you allow your mind and body to relax, helping to release tension and anxiety. This stress reduction can improve mood and energy levels, making it easier to handle daily challenges. Self-care also enhances self-esteem. When you prioritize your well-being, you send a message to yourself that you are valuable and deserving of care. This boost in self-worth can have a positive ripple effect on other areas of your life, including relationships and work. By taking care of yourself, you prevent burnout. Constantly pushing yourself without breaks can lead to physical and emotional exhaustion—regular self-care acts as a buffer, replenishing your energy and resilience.

Creating a personalized self-care routine starts with identifying activities that bring you joy and relaxation. Think about what makes you feel happy and calm. It could be reading a book, walking in nature, or spending time with loved ones. Once you've identified these activities, set aside dedicated time for them. Schedule self-care just like you would any other necessary appointment. This could be a daily practice, like a morning meditation session, or a weekly ritual, like a Sunday evening bubble bath. Balancing physical, emotional, and mental self-care activities ensures a holistic approach. Physical self-care might include regular exercise, such as yoga or jogging, and healthy eating. Emotional self-care could involve journaling to process your feelings, talking to a therapist, or engaging in hobbies that make you feel fulfilled. Mental self-care includes activities that stimulate your mind, like reading, solving puzzles, or practicing meditation.

Maintaining consistency in your self-care routine can be challenging but essential for long-term benefits. Creating a self-care schedule helps establish a routine. Write your self-care activities in a planner or set reminders on your phone. These reminders make it easier to stick to your plan and ensure you remember to take time for yourself. Setting reminders is another helpful strategy. Use alarms or notifications to prompt you to take breaks and engage in self-care activities. Involving loved ones in your self-care can also be beneficial. Share your self-care goals with friends or family and encourage them to join you. Having this support system makes the activities more enjoyable and provides accountability.

Different types of self-care activities cater to various aspects of your well-being. Physical self-care involves actions that keep your body healthy and energized. Include regular exercise to release endorphins, boost mood, and healthy eating, providing the nutrients your body needs to function optimally. Emotional self-care focuses on nurturing your emotional health. Writing in a journal helps you process complex feelings and find clarity about your thoughts and experiences. Therapy offers a safe space to explore your feelings and develop coping strategies. Mental self-care involves engaging in activities that stimulate your mind and promote relaxation. Reading can transport you to different worlds and provide new perspectives. Meditation helps calm the mind and reduce stress, fostering a sense of inner peace.

Self-Care Checklist

Here's a simple checklist to help you develop and maintain your self-care routine:

- Identify activities that bring you joy and relaxation
- Set aside dedicated time for self-care
- Balance physical, emotional, and mental self-care activities
- Create a self-care schedule
- Set reminders for self-care activities
- Involve loved ones in your self-care routine

When you consistently practice self-care activities in your daily routine, you build a strong foundation for emotional growth and stability. It's about committing yourself, acknowledging your worth, and taking steps to ensure your well-being.

Ongoing Personal Development Practices

Imagine this: you're in your mid-twenties, navigating a new career while trying to build meaningful relationships. You can quickly feel overwhelmed, thinking others expect you to have everything figured out. But personal development isn't about achieving perfection; it's about continuous growth. Ongoing self-improvement promotes self-awareness, allowing you better to understand your strengths, weaknesses, and triggers. By enhancing your skills and competencies, you become more adept at handling life's challenges, whether they're in your personal or professional life. A growth mindset fosters resilience, helping you view setbacks as learning opportunities rather than failures.

Numerous personal development practices can support your growth. Setting and pursuing individual goals is fundamental. Start by identifying your goals in life, career, relationships, or personal well-being. Engaging in lifelong learning through courses and workshops keeps your mind active and opens new avenues for growth. Whether it's a weekend workshop on emotional intelligence or a night class in creative writing, these activities stimulate your mind and broaden your horizons. Seeking feedback and mentorship provides you with invaluable insights and guidance. A mentor can help you navigate complex situations and offer perspectives you might have overlooked.

Setting personal development goals is crucial to make them realistic and achievable. Using SMART criteria can help. Your goals should be Specific, Measurable, Achievable, Relevant, and Time-bound. For example, rather than setting a vague goal like "improve communication skills," try "attend a communication workshop by the end of the month." Breaking goals into manageable steps makes them less daunting and more attainable. If you want to run a marathon, start with shorter runs and gradually increase your distance. Tracking progress and celebrating milestones keeps you motivated. Keep a journal or use an app to record your achievements and reflect on your journey.

Victoria, a 28-year-old marketing associate felt stagnate in her career. She initiated the help of a coach and identified public speaking as a critical skill holding her back from advancement opportunities. Together, they developed a structured plan to address this limitation.

They began by setting clear, measurable goals. Victoria committed to giving one presentation per week, starting with small groups and gradually increasing audience size. To support this, she enrolled in a 12-week public speaking course, which provided her with foundational techniques and regular practice opportunities.

Alongside formal training, Victoria implemented daily exercises. She practiced vocal warm-ups, recorded herself speaking, and analyzed her body language in front of a mirror. To combat her anxiety, they incorporated mindfulness techniques, including deep breathing exercises and positive visualization before presentations.

Victoria also leveraged her professional network. She sought feedback from a senior colleague who became her mentor, providing invaluable industry-specific advice. Additionally, she organized a small group of peers for weekly practice sessions, creating a supportive environment for mutual growth.

Over six months, Victoria's progress was remarkable. Her confidence in presentations increased significantly, as evidenced by positive feedback from colleagues and superiors. This newfound skill led to her taking on project lead roles, where she could showcase her improved communication abilities.

The impact extended beyond her career. Victoria reported increased self-esteem and willingness to voice her opinions in various settings. She even volunteered to speak at a local community event, something she would have never considered before.

Victoria's case illustrates the transformative power of focused personal development. By identifying a specific area for improvement, creating a multi-faceted approach, and consistently applying effort, she not only enhanced her professional prospects but also experienced significant personal growth.

John, a 32-year-old software developer, had struggled with social anxiety for most of his adult life. His discomfort in social situations had limited his personal relationships and professional opportunities. Recognizing the need for change, John set a goal to improve his social comfort and confidence.

He began his journey by creating a graduated exposure plan. John started with small, low-pressure social interactions, such as brief conversations with colleagues during lunch breaks. He set weekly goals, gradually increasing the duration and complexity of his social engagements.

To support his efforts, John sought the guidance of a mentor who had overcome similar challenges. This mentor provided strategies for managing anxiety and offered encouragement throughout the process. Together, they developed coping mechanisms, including deep breathing exercises and positive self-talk, which John could employ in challenging situations.

John also committed to attending one social event per month, starting with small gatherings of close friends. He prepared for these events by visualizing positive outcomes and reminding himself of past successes. After each event, he reflected on his experiences, noting areas of improvement and challenges to address.

John's comfort in social settings noticeably improved over a period of several months. He initiated conversations more frequently and experienced less anticipatory anxiety before events.

His increased confidence led to more active participation in team meetings at work, resulting in new project opportunities. He also reported feeling more fulfilled in his personal life, having formed deeper connections with friends and even starting to date.

John's case demonstrates how structured goal-setting, gradual exposure, and consistent effort can lead to significant improvements in managing social anxiety. His success underscores the importance of patience, self-compassion, and support in overcoming long-standing social challenges.

It's essential to recognize that personal development is an ongoing process. There will always be areas to improve and new skills to learn. Embrace this journey with an open mind and a willingness to grow. Participate in activities that challenge you and urge you out of your comfort zone. Reflect on your experiences and learn from them. Seek opportunities for growth, whether through formal education, mentorship, or personal exploration. Surround yourself with supportive people who encourage your development and celebrate your achievements.

As you continue on this path of personal development, remember to be patient with yourself. Growth takes time, and it's okay to progress at your own pace. Celebrate your small wins and use them as motivation to keep going. Reflect on your journey regularly and adjust your goals as needed. Personal development is not about reaching an outcome; it's about aspiring to become the best version of yourself. Keep pushing forward, stay curious, and embrace the endless possibilities for growth.

Cultivating Emotional Resilience

Emotional resilience is adapting to stress and adversity and maintaining stability even when life throws curveballs. It's about bouncing back from challenges stronger and more capable. Think of it as a psychological immune system that helps you deal with difficulties without crumbling. Emotional resilience is crucial because it allows you to navigate life's ups and downs without losing balance. It helps maintain emotional stability, ensuring you don't get swept away by every emotional wave. Moreover, it enhances problem-solving skills, enabling you to approach challenges with a clear mind and a steady heart.

Building emotional resilience involves practical exercises and strategies. Mindfulness and meditation practices are powerful tools. They help you stay present, reducing the tendency to regret past mistakes or worry about the future. Start with simple mindfulness exercises like deep breathing or body scanning. Spend a few minutes daily focusing on your breathing, noticing how you feel as you inhale and exhale. Meditation can also be a valuable practice. Even a short daily session can help calm your mind and improve your emotional stability. Cognitive-behavioral strategies are another practical approach. These techniques involve identifying and challenging negative thought patterns. For example, if you think, "I can't handle this," reframe it to, "I can find a way to manage this situation." This change in perspective can considerably impact your emotional resilience. Building a solid support network is equally important. Surround yourself with people who uplift and support you. Having a trusted circle to turn to during tough times can make a difference.

Self-compassion plays a vital role in emotional resilience. It's about being kind to yourself, especially when things go wrong. Reducing self-criticism is a crucial aspect. Instead of berating yourself up over mistakes, practice self-compassion. Remind yourself that everyone makes mistakes and that it's okay to be imperfect. Promote positive self-talk by replacing negative thoughts with encouraging ones. For instance, if you're feeling down, tell yourself, "I'm doing my best, and that's enough." Encouraging self-care is another crucial element. Taking time to nurture yourself emotionally, physically, and mentally can significantly boost your resilience. Engage in activities that make you feel good, whether walking in nature, reading a book, or spending time with loved ones.

Real-life examples can illustrate the benefits of emotional resilience. Harper, a 32-year-old marketing professional, was blindsided by a layoff after five years with her firm. Initially overwhelmed by anxiety and self-doubt, Harper took a proactive approach to managing her stress. She began a daily mindfulness practice, starting with just ten minutes each morning using a meditation app. Simultaneously, she activated her support network, reaching out to friends and family for emotional support and perspective. This combination helped Harper gradually shift from a state of panic to one of openness to new possibilities.

As her anxiety decreased, Harper made a pivotal decision to invest in herself, using part of her severance to enroll in a graphic design course she'd long been interested in. This move not only occupied her time productively but also expanded her skill set. Over the following months, she noticed a marked change in her outlook. She approached job interviews with newfound calmness and purpose, no longer fixated on recreating her old role but excited about potential new paths.

Six months post-layoff, Harper secured a position at a design studio that allowed her to combine her marketing background with her newly acquired design skills. Harper's case illustrates how mindfulness practices, social support, and a willingness to acquire new skills can transform a career crisis into an opportunity for growth. Harper not only found new employment but also reported greater job satisfaction and a sense of personal development, demonstrating the potential for positive outcomes even in challenging professional circumstances.

Paul's case is a testament to the effectiveness of cognitive-behavioral strategies in managing social anxiety. Paul, a 34-year-old software engineer, had long grappled with intense social anxiety that significantly impacted his personal and professional life. When he first sought help, Paul reported avoiding most social situations and experiencing severe distress when forced to interact in group settings.

The treatment plan focused on three key areas: challenging negative thoughts, building confidence through gradual exposure, and developing a supportive network. Paul's doctor guided him through cognitive restructuring exercises, helping him identify and reframe his anxious thoughts. For instance, Paul learned to question his assumption that others were constantly judging him negatively.

Simultaneously, Paul embarked on a series of graduated exposure exercises. He started with low-stress situations, such as brief interactions with cashiers, and progressively worked up to attending larger social gatherings. His doctor noted that Paul's commitment to these exercises, despite initial discomfort, was crucial to his progress.

As part of building his support system, Paul joined a social anxiety support group. This not only provided him with a safe space to practice social skills but also connected him with others who understood his struggles.

Over six months, Paul observed significant improvements in his emotional resilience. He reported feeling more at ease in social situations and even began to enjoy interactions that previously terrified him. A notable milestone was Paul's voluntary participation in a work presentation, something he had always avoided before.

Paul's case illustrates how a multi-faceted approach to social anxiety, combining cognitive techniques, behavioral strategies, and social support, can lead to substantial improvements in quality of life. While Paul continues to work on his anxiety, his progress demonstrates the potential for overcoming long-standing social fears and building genuine confidence in social situations.

Emotional resilience is often a focus in therapy sessions. Therapists work with clients to develop strategies for managing stress and adversity. For instance, in cognitive-behavioral therapy (CBT), clients learn to identify and challenge negative thought patterns. They practice reframing these thoughts into more positive and realistic perspectives. Therapists also use techniques like exposure therapy to help clients build resilience by gradually facing their fears. These therapeutic approaches can significantly enhance emotional resilience, providing the tools for people to successfully navigate life's challenges.

Emotional resilience is not about eliminating stress or adversity. Instead, it's about developing the capacity to deal with these challenges healthily and constructively. It's about bouncing back from setbacks and growing stronger with each experience. With mindfulness, cognitive-behavioral strategies, self-compassion, and a strong support network, you can cultivate emotional resilience and handle life's ups and downs with greater ease and confidence.

Recognizing and Avoiding Toxic Relationship Patterns

Have you ever found yourself in a relationship where something feels off, but you can't quite put your finger on it? Recognizing and avoiding toxic relationship patterns is crucial for your emotional well-being. In toxic relationships, one partner emotionally manipulates the other, wielding control through guilt-tripping, gaslighting, or passive-aggressive behaviors. This manipulation creates a power imbalance, leaving you feeling trapped and powerless. A lack of respect and support is another hallmark of a toxic relationship. If your partner frequently dismisses your feelings, belittles your achievements, or fails to support your endeavors, these are red flags. Consistent negativity and conflict also indicate toxicity. When every conversation seems to turn into an argument, or when you constantly feel drained and on edge, it's a sign that the relationship is harming your mental health.

Toxic relationships profoundly impact your emotional well-being. Increased anxiety and depression are expected outcomes. The constant stress and emotional turmoil can exacerbate existing mental health conditions or even trigger new ones. Over time, your self-esteem can take a significant hit. When your partner constantly criticizes or dismisses your feelings, you internalize these negative messages. You start doubting your worth and questioning your judgment. This damaged self-esteem spills over into other aspects of your life. You may struggle to make decisions at work, hesitate to voice your opinions with friends, or find it hard to form new relationships. The persistent self-doubt makes it challenging to trust your instincts or to believe that others genuinely value you. Emotional exhaustion is another consequence. The relentless cycle of conflict, manipulation, and negativity can leave you feeling utterly drained, with little energy for anything else. This exhaustion can spill over into your work, social life, and other relationships, creating a pervasive sense of burnout.

Recognizing toxic relationship patterns involves a few key strategies. Start by reflecting on your relationship dynamics. Take a step back and objectively assess your interactions with your partner. Are there consistent patterns of behavior that leave you feeling upset or diminished? Writing down these observations can help clarify your thoughts. Seeking feedback from trusted friends or therapists can provide an external perspective. Sometimes, being in the thick of it makes it hard to see the complete picture. Friends and therapists can offer insights that you might have overlooked. Observing patterns of behavior over time is crucial. Toxic behaviors often follow a cycle—recognizing these patterns can help you understand the extent of the toxicity. Keep a journal to track these behaviors, noting recurring issues or conflicts.

If you identify toxic patterns, taking actionable steps to protect yourself is essential. Setting and enforcing boundaries is the first step. Communicate your limits to your partner and stick to them. For example, if your partner frequently belittles you, tell them that this behavior is unacceptable and that you'll leave the conversation if it continues. Consistently enforcing these boundaries is critical to maintaining your well-being. Seeking professional support can provide additional guidance and validation. A therapist can help you navigate the complexities of the relationship and offer strategies for managing toxic behaviors. Prioritizing self-care and well-being is paramount. Engage in activities that nurture your mind and body, whether spending time with supportive friends, engaging in hobbies, or practicing mindfulness. These activities can help replenish your emotional reserves and build resilience.

Leaving a toxic relationship can be daunting, but it's sometimes necessary for your mental health. Start by creating a safety plan. If you feel unsafe, have a trusted friend or family member you can stay with. Gradually distance yourself from the toxic partner, reducing contact and setting firm boundaries. Write down your reasons for leaving as a reminder during moments of doubt. Surround yourself with a strong support network. Friends, family, and support groups can provide your needed encouragement and strength. Finally, focus on rebuilding your self-esteem. Engage in activities that make you feel good about yourself and remind you of your worth. It's a challenging process, but your well-being is worth the effort.

Recognizing and avoiding toxic relationship patterns is essential for your mental and emotional health. You can identify toxic elements by reflecting on your relationship dynamics, seeking feedback, and observing behavior patterns. Taking actionable steps like setting boundaries, seeking professional support, and prioritizing self-care can help you navigate and, if necessary, exit these harmful relationships. Your well-being should always be a priority, and taking these steps can lead to healthier, more fulfilling connections.

Celebrating Progress and Small Wins

Imagine finally reaching the top of a hill after a long, challenging climb. The sense of accomplishment is exhilarating and motivates you to tackle the next challenge. Celebrating progress, no matter how small, is crucial for sustained growth. Acknowledging and celebrating small achievements builds motivation and momentum. It creates a positive feedback loop, where each success fuels the desire to achieve more. Enhancing self-esteem is another significant benefit. When you take the time to recognize your accomplishments, you reinforce the belief that you are capable and worthy. This boost in self-worth can have a profound impact on your overall well-being. Celebrating progress also reinforces positive behaviors, making it more likely that you will continue to engage in actions that contribute to your growth and happiness.

Recognizing and celebrating small wins involves setting and tracking small, achievable goals. Break down larger objectives into smaller, manageable tasks. For instance, if your goal is to improve communication in your relationship, start with a daily practice of active listening. Track your progress by noting each time you successfully engage in this practice. Reflecting on daily or weekly accomplishments helps you see the incremental steps you are taking toward your larger goals. At the end of each day or week, take a moment to reflect on what you've achieved. Even small steps are worth celebrating, like having a meaningful conversation with your partner or taking a walk to clear your mind. Sharing successes with supportive friends or partners can amplify the positive effects. When you share your achievements, you invite others to celebrate with you, creating a sense of community and mutual encouragement.

There are many ways to celebrate progress, and finding methods that resonate with you is essential. Rewarding yourself with enjoyable activities is a simple yet effective way to celebrate. This could be anything from treating yourself to your favorite meal, taking a relaxing bath, or spending a day doing something you love. Creating a visual progress tracker can also be motivating. Use a chart, journal, or app to track your achievements. Seeing your progress visually can remind you how far you've come. Hosting a small celebration or gathering with friends or loved ones is another beautiful way to acknowledge your progress. It doesn't have to be elaborate—a simple get-together to share your success and enjoy each other's company can be incredibly fulfilling.

Let me share a personal anecdote. When I first started working on managing my anxiety, I set a goal to practice mindfulness for at least five minutes each day. Initially, it seemed like a small step, but it was challenging to find consistency. I created a progress tracker, marking each day I successfully practiced mindfulness. Seeing the streak of consecutive days grow was incredibly motivating. I also shared my progress with a close friend, who celebrated each milestone. One month later, we hosted a small gathering to celebrate the achievement. The support and recognition from my friend made the journey feel less lonely and more rewarding.

Similarly, consider the story of Ethan, who struggled with low self-esteem. He set a goal to write down three things he appreciated about himself each day. At first, it felt awkward and forced, but he committed to the practice. Over time, he noticed a shift in his self-perception. To celebrate his progress, he treated himself to a weekend getaway, something he had always wanted to do but never felt he deserved. This celebration reinforced his newfound self-worth and motivated him to continue practicing self-appreciation.

Celebrating small wins might seem insignificant, but it can profoundly impact your emotional growth and well-being. It's about recognizing that every step forward is a victory, no matter how small. You build a foundation of positivity and motivation by setting achievable goals, reflecting on your progress, and celebrating your achievements. These small celebrations create moments of joy and recognition, reinforcing the belief that you are capable and worthy of success. Embrace these moments, share them with loved ones, and let them fuel your journey toward sustained emotional growth and healthy relationships.

Creating a Vision for Your Future Relationships

Having a clear vision for your future relationships is like having a roadmap that guides you toward fulfilling and meaningful connections. This vision provides direction and purpose, helping you make intentional choices that align with your values and goals. Knowing what you want in a relationship, you can navigate your romantic life with greater clarity and confidence. A relationship vision also enhances relationship satisfaction. It ensures that you and your partner are on the same page, working towards common goals and values, which fosters a more profound sense of connection and fulfillment.

To create a meaningful relationship vision, reflect on your past relationship experiences. What worked well, and what didn't? What patterns do you notice, and what lessons have you learned? This reflection helps you identify what you truly want and need in a relationship. Next, consider your core values and priorities. What qualities are non-negotiable in a partner? What kind of life do you envision together? These values will serve as the foundation of your relationship vision. Setting specific relationship goals is also crucial. Think about what you want to achieve in your relationship, such as building a solid emotional connection, maintaining open communication, or supporting each other's personal growth. Be as specific as possible to create a clear and actionable vision.

Aligning your actions with your relationship vision requires ongoing effort and intentionality. Start by communicating your vision with potential partners. Share your values, goals, and what you're looking for in a relationship early on. This transparency helps ensure that both of you are on the same page and can work towards a shared vision. Making intentional choices in dating and relationships is also essential. Choose partners who align with your vision and values, and be mindful of your actions and decisions. Regularly revisiting and adjusting your vision is crucial for staying on track. Your vision may change as you grow and evolve, and that's okay. Reflect on your relationship vision periodically and make adjustments as needed to ensure it continues to align with your values and goals.

Consider the story of Laura and Mike, who created a shared relationship vision early in their dating journey. They valued personal growth and open communication and set specific goals to support each other's dreams and maintain a solid emotional connection. Regularly discussing and adjusting their vision as needed, they built a fulfilling and supportive relationship that aligned with their values and goals. Another example is Jenna, who, after several challenging relationships, decided to create a clear vision for her future relationships. She reflected on her past experiences, identified her core values of trust and respect, and set specific goals to build a relationship based on these principles. By aligning her actions with her vision, Jenna found a partner who shared her values and built a meaningful and fulfilling relationship.

Creating a vision for future relationships is a powerful tool for building fulfilling and meaningful connections. You can navigate your romantic life with greater clarity and confidence by reflecting on past experiences, identifying core values, setting specific goals, and aligning your actions with your vision. Regularly revisiting and adjusting your vision ensures it continues aligning with your evolving values and goals. Embrace the process of creating and living your relationship vision, and you'll find yourself building relationships that are deeply satisfying and aligned with your true self.

Remember, Your Voice Matters!

If you found value in this book, please consider taking a moment to leave a review. Your words can inspire others on their journey to overcome relationship anxiety and overthinking. A simple, honest review on Amazon can make a world of difference.

Thank you for being part of this community of growth and healing. Your experience could be the encouragement someone else needs to take their first step towards change.

With deepest appreciation,

Cynthia Shepherd

Scan the QR code above with the camera on your phone or tap here:
https://www.amazon.com/review/
review-your-purchases/?asin=B0DJ2WPR3J

CONCLUSION

A Moment to Reflect on Key Insights and Tools

As we reach the end of our journey together, let's take a moment to reflect on the key insights and tools we've explored. We began by understanding relationship anxiety and overthinking, shedding light on how these issues can infiltrate your life and relationships. We delved into the root causes, such as attachment styles and past traumas, and examined the emotional and behavioral symptoms that accompany them.

We then moved on to building self-awareness and self-compassion. You learned how to quiet your inner critic and embrace your true self through mindfulness practices, journaling, and positive affirmations. We discussed the importance of recognizing and celebrating your strengths and how daily self-compassion techniques can foster emotional resilience.

Healing from past traumas was another crucial step. We explored methods for recognizing and validating your trauma, processing emotional pain, and using guided visualizations to promote healing. Seeking professional help was emphasized, along with strategies for releasing emotional baggage and rebuilding trust after betrayal.

Managing social anxiety in romantic contexts was also covered, providing practical exercises and coping strategies to build confidence in social situations. We discussed the benefits of gradual exposure, role-playing scenarios, and various techniques for easing anxiety before and during dates.

Developing secure attachment styles formed the backbone of building healthier relationships. We examined the different attachment styles and provided actionable steps to transition from anxious or avoidant attachment to secure attachment. Through real-life examples and practical exercises, you saw how self-awareness and self-compassion play pivotal roles in this transformation.

Effective communication and setting boundaries were highlighted as essential for maintaining healthy relationships. Active listening, expressing needs without fear, and conflict resolution techniques were discussed in detail. You learned to set and maintain boundaries, ensuring your relationships are rooted in mutual respect and understanding.

Finally, we focused on sustaining emotional growth and healthy relationships. From developing a self-care routine to ongoing personal development practices, you were equipped with tools to cultivate emotional resilience. Recognizing and avoiding toxic relationship patterns, celebrating progress, and creating a vision for future relationships were critical elements for long-term well-being.

The key takeaways from this book revolve around self-awareness, self-compassion, and practical strategies for emotional growth. Understanding the root causes of your anxieties and overthinking allows you to address them effectively. Building self-awareness through mindfulness and journaling helps you recognize patterns and triggers. Practicing self-compassion fosters a kinder relationship with yourself, reducing self-criticism and promoting emotional resilience. Setting boundaries and communicating effectively pave the way for healthier relationships.

Now, it's time for a call to action. Take the tools and insights you've gained from this book and put them into practice. Start small, focusing on one area at a time. Whether practicing daily affirmations, setting boundaries, or seeking professional help, every step brings you closer to emotional well-being and healthier relationships. Remember, change doesn't happen overnight, but you can transform your life with persistence and dedication.

As someone who has walked this path, I know your challenges. I've been there, feeling overwhelmed by anxiety and crippled by self-doubt. But I also know the incredible transformation possible when you commit to healing and growth. You have the strength and resilience within you to overcome these challenges. Believe in yourself and trust the process.

In closing, I want to leave you with a final encouragement. You are worthy of love, respect, and happiness. Your journey toward emotional growth and healthier relationships is a testament to your courage and determination. Embrace each step, celebrate your progress, and never lose sight of your worth. The path to emotional freedom is a journey, not a destination. Keep moving forward, and remember that you are not alone. With each small step, you are creating a brighter, more fulfilling future for yourself. Thank you for allowing me to be a part of your journey.

BIBLIOGRAPHY

Allen, R. K. (n.d.). Toxic relationship patterns that kill love. Roger K Allen. https://www.rogerkallen.com/toxic-relationship-patterns-that-kill-love/

Calm. (n.d.). How to set personal development goals for your life and work. https://www.calm.com/blog/personal-development-goals

Calm. (n.d.). Negative self-talk: 8 ways to quiet your inner critic. https://www.calm.com/blog/negative-self-talk

Cherry, K. (2023, May 15). How to practice exposure therapy for social anxiety. Verywell Mind. https://www.verywellmind.com/practice-social-anxiety-disorder-exposure-therapy-3024845

Cherry, K. (2023, August 14). Social anxiety coping skills: Best self-help strategies. Verywell Mind. https://www.verywellmind.com/coping-with-social-anxiety-disorder-3024836

Choosing Therapy. (2023, September 1). Dating with social anxiety: 7 Tips from a therapist. https://www.choosingtherapy.com/dating-with-social-anxiety/

Cuncic, A. (2023, September 13). Coping with insecurity in a relationship. Verywell Mind. https://www.verywellmind.com/coping-with-insecurity-in-a-relationship-5207949

Curology. (n.d.). How to create a self-care routine that actually sticks. https://curology.com/blog/how-to-plan-a-self-care-routine/

Forbes Health. (2023, July 19). Relationship anxiety: Causes, signs and how to overcome it. https://www.forbes.com/health/mind/relationship-anxiety/

Gagnon, S. (2022, July 11). How to use journaling to cope with PTSD. Verywell Mind. https://www.verywellmind.com/how-to-use-journaling-to-cope-with-ptsd-2797594

HelpGuide. (n.d.). Attachment styles and how they affect adult relationships. https://www.helpguide.org/articles/relationships-communication/attachment-and-adult-relationships.htm

HelpGuide. (n.d.). Setting healthy boundaries in relationships. https://
www.helpguide.org/articles/relationships-communication/setting-healthy-
boundaries-in-relationships.htm

Holding Hope Marriage & Family Therapy. (n.d.). Active listening in
relationships: A path to deeper intimacy. https://holdinghopemft.com/
active-listening-a-key-to-deeper-intimacy-and-understanding-in-your-
relationship/

Jorel, J. (2022, April 24). Reforming my attachment style. From anxious-
avoidant to secure. Medium. https://jemmajorel.medium.com/reforming-
my-attachment-style-674074226185

Mindful. (2022, August 10). How to navigate overthinking with
compassionate awareness. https://www.mindful.org/how-to-navigate-
overthinking-with-compassionate-awareness/

Neff, K. (n.d.). Self-compassion practices: Cultivate inner peace and joy.
Self-Compassion. https://self-compassion.org/self-compassion-practices/

Positive Psychology. (n.d.). 21 Mindfulness exercises & activities for
adults (+ PDF). https://positivepsychology.com/mindfulness-exercises-
techniques-activities/

Positive Psychology. (n.d.). 8 Attachment style questionnaires & tests to
assess clients. https://positivepsychology.com/attachment-style-tests/

Positive Psychology. (n.d.). Conflict resolution in relationships &
couples: 5 Strategies. https://positivepsychology.com/conflict-resolution-
relationships/

Positive Psychology. (n.d.). Guided imagery in therapy: 20 Powerful
scripts and techniques. https://positivepsychology.com/guided-imagery-
scripts/

Positive Psychology. (n.d.). Role play in therapy: 21 Scripts & examples
for your sessions. https://positivepsychology.com/role-playing-scripts/

Positive Psychology. (n.d.). What is emotional resilience? (+6 Proven ways
to build it). https://positivepsychology.com/emotional-resilience/

Psychcentral. (2022, November 23). 64 Journaling prompts for self-
discovery. https://psychcentral.com/blog/ready-set-journal-64-journaling-
prompts-for-self-discovery

Psychology Today. (2023, July 25). How to rebuild trust after betrayal in a relationship. https://www.psychologytoday.com/us/blog/the-discomfort-zone/202407/how-to-rebuild-trust-after-betrayal-in-a-relationship-0

Raypole, C. (2023, July 3). Self-reflection: Benefits and how to practice. Verywell Mind. https://www.verywellmind.com/self-reflection-importance-benefits-and-strategies-7500858

Ronen, D. (2018, September 25). Give yourself a break: The power of self-compassion. Harvard Business Review. https://hbr.org/2018/09/give-yourself-a-break-the-power-of-self-compassion

Seattle Christian Counseling. (n.d.). 7 Keys to effective communication skills in relationships. https://seattlechristiancounseling.com/articles/7-keys-to-effective-communication-skills-in-relationships

Shern, A. L. (2023, July 3). Relationship trauma: Signs, causes, how to heal. Verywell Health. https://www.verywellhealth.com/relationship-trauma-5211576

Staik, A. (n.d.). Cognitive distortions in relationships | Thought patterns. Cognitive Behavioral Therapy Center. https://cogbtherapy.com/cbt-blog/cognitive-distortions-in-relationships

Tanner, L. (2018). The effect of positive affirmations on self-esteem and well-being [Senior thesis, Dominican University of California]. Scholar Works @ Dominican. https://scholar.dominican.edu/cgi/viewcontent.cgi?article=1010&context=psychology-senior-theses

Zamosky, L. (n.d.). How to harness the power of visualization for self-improvement. BetterHelp. https://www.betterhelp.com/advice/visualization/how-to-harness-the-power-of-visualization-for-self-improvement/

Zarrella, S. M., & Scherer, L. D. (2021). A review of attachment theory in the context of adolescent parenting. Maternal and Child Health Journal, 25(1), 19-31. https://www.ncbi.nlm.nih.gov/pmc/articles/PMC3051370/

Made in the USA
Las Vegas, NV
17 January 2025